THE CHARLES DICKENS—THOMAS POWELL VENDETTA

The Story in Documents

THE CHARLES DICKENS— THOMAS POWELL VENDETTA

The Story in Documents

by

Sidney P. Moss and Carolyn J. Moss

The Whitston Publishing Company
Troy, New York
1996

Library of Congress Catalog Card Number 95-2175

ISBN 0-87875-475-X

Printed in the United States of America

To Angela Rubin

and

Deborah Cordts

For librarianship of extraordinary intelligence and imagination, performed with perfect good nature

ALSO BY SIDNEY P. MOSS

CHARLES DICKENS' QUARREL WITH AMERICA

CHARLES DICKENS AND HIS CHICAGO RELATIVES
A Documentary Narrative
(with Carolyn J. Moss)

POE'S LITERARY BATTLES
The Critic in the Context of His Literary Milieu

POE'S MAJOR CRISIS
His Libel Suit and New York's Literary World

HAWTHORNE AND MELVILLE
An Inquiry into Their Art and the Mystery of Their Friendship

ALSO BY CAROLYN J. MOSS

CHARLES DICKENS AND HIS CHICAGO RELATIVES
A Documentary Narrative
(with Sidney P. Moss)

KATE FIELD: SELECTED LETTERS

BIBLIOGRAPHIC GUIDE TO SELF-DISCLOSURE LITERATURE

THE NEW COMPOSITION BY LOGIC
(with Sidney P. Moss)

CONTENTS

LIST OF ILLUSTRATIONS

PREFACE AND ACKNOWLEDGMENTS

The vendetta recreated here engaged Charles Dickens, on and off, for three years (though he had known Thomas Powell for almost a decade), and often enough his dander was riz by it, to use his expression in *Martin Chuzzlewit*. As any Dickensian could have predicted, the Master had no intention of yielding an inch to his antagonist, let alone of being bested by him. Thus the feud occupied him in letters and even moved him to enlist allies on both sides of the Atlantic. Of far greater consequence, Dickens was so absorbed by the vendetta that he drew upon it for various narrative purposes in the three novels he wrote during its course.

Despite its biographical and literary importance, the information concerning this vendetta has been of a fragmentary, though tantalizing, nature. Our purpose, therefore, was twofold: to collect all the documents relevant to the vendetta and to present them in their Victorian context so that the feud can regain its pristine colors while its revelations are disclosed.

Not every document was found, of course, for old records have ways of disappearing—the worst way, perhaps, that of being lost in the very archives designed to preserve and make them available. In such instances our failed efforts at recovery were noted, if only to spare other researchers needless frustration. By sheer good luck, however, most of our efforts were successful and led to the well-known heart-stirring delights of research: the discoveries of old court records, death certificates, wills, unpublished manuscript letters, items in defunct magazines and newspapers—all those rare, odd artefacts that suddenly and wonderfully explain a mystery.

Needless to say, little done here could have been accomplished without the work of other scholars, and our debts to them are duly recorded in the text and in "Works Cited." But certainly, nothing whatever could have been accomplished without the cooperation of the institutions and the large-hearted individuals here named:

A. Bailey of the British Library, **James R. Sewell**, City Archivist for the Corporation of London Records Office, **Samuel Jones**, Head Archivist of the Greater London Record Office, **Oliver Harris**, Archivist for the London Borough of Croydon, the unnamed **Borough Archivist** of the Hackney Archives Department, **D. B. Robinson**, County Archivist for Surrey County Council, and **Nigel Taylor**, Reader Services Department of the Public Record Office, London, for attempts to secure records of Croydon Magistrates Court and of Miles Lunatic Asylum concerning Thomas Powell;

Sally Brown, Curator of Literary Manuscripts, The British Library, and **Karen Lightner**, Reference Librarian, Rare Book Department, The Free Library of Philadelphia, for answering questions concerning the so-called "Proof";

The British Library's Newspaper Library for miscellaneous newspaper items;

Kenneth R. Cobb, Director of the New York Department of Records and Information Services, Municipal Archives, for searching the Indictment Files and Minutes of the Court of General Sessions, as well as the Docket Books of the New York Police Courts, for records in Thomas Powell's libel suit against Lewis Gaylord Clark.

Barbara Jones, Information Officer & Archivist, Lloyd's Register of Shipping, for valuable information about Thomas Chapman, and **J. S. Curtis** of Lloyd's Information Centre, for a photograph of a painting of Thomas Chapman;

J. Mark Kressenberg, Attorney-at-Law, for valuable suggestions and for referral to pertinent legal works;

The Library of Congress, especially its Newspaper Department and its Photoduplication Service;

Myles McKenna, Clerk of County, Civil Court of the City of New York, for directing us to the Division of Old Records in search of Thomas Powell's lawsuits, and **Joseph Van Nostrand**, County Clerk and Clerk of the Supreme Court, New York County Court House, for locating the documents in Powell's libel suit against Hiram Fuller;

New Jersey State Bureau of Vital Statistics for the death certificate of Thomas Powell;

Oxford University Press for quotations from the Pilgrim Edition of *The Letters of Charles Dickens,* edited by Madeline House, Graham Storey, and Kathleen Tillotson, the General Editors, as well as by K. J. Fielding, Nina Burgis, and Angus Easson. Reprinted by permission of Oxford University Press;

Wilfred Partington for "Should a Biographer Tell?" and the **Editors of the Pilgrim Edition** of the Dickens letters (especially **Kathleen Tillotson**) for pointing the way, though we traveled by our own independent itinerary;

Record Keeper's Department, Principal Registry of the Family Division, Somerset House, London, for the Last Will and Testament of Thomas Chapman;

Jean Rainwater, Coordinator of Reader Service, John Hay Library, Brown University Library, for transcribing five Thomas Powell letters addressed to Colonel Rush C. Hawkins during the American Civil War;

Debra Randorf, Reference Librarian, The New-York Historical Society, for miscellaneous services;

Nancy L. Romero, Head, Rare Book and Special Collections Library, University of Illinois at Urbana-Champaign, for searching the Richard Bentley Archives for items relating to Powell's *Living Authors of England;*

John D. Stinson, Manuscripts Specialist, for copies of the Thomas Powell letters in the Duyckinck Family Papers, Rare Books and Manuscripts Division, The New York Public Library, Astor, Lenox and Tilden Foundation, and **Wayne Furman**, Office of Special Collections, for permission to quote two passages from them;

Graham Storey and **Kathleen Tillotson**, General Editors of the Pilgrim Edition of the Dickens letters, for answers to various queries;

Jennifer A. Watts, Associate Curator of Photographs, Huntington Library, San Marino, California, for sending a photograph of Dickens, and **William A. Moffett**, Director of the Library, for permission to reproduce it.

INTRODUCTION

During what was arguably his most creative and active period (*Dombey and Son, David Copperfield,* and *Bleak House*), Charles Dickens became fast friends with and a bitter enemy of Thomas Powell, raconteur, wit, and charmer whose genius lay in cultivating the genius of the age—among them William Wordsworth, Leigh Hunt, Walter Savage Landor, Elizabeth Barrett, and Robert Browning. When Powell, to his friends' wonderment, was exposed as an embezzler, forger, and confidence man, Dickens, instead of condemning him, was touched by his tragedy, especially when the man attempted suicide and was committed to a madhouse in order to escape transportation or prison. Indeed, Powell's plight was such as to move Dickens to invoke Christ's prayer, "Lead us not into temptation."

But the novelist's compassion turned to anger when the man he considered his friend, having fled the madhouse and escaped to New York, proceeded to abuse him at length in his *Living Authors of England* for modeling Paul Dombey on Powell's uncle Thomas Chapman and, in the process, as Powell put it, "grossly caricaturing" him. For Thomas Chapman was, in addition to being Dickens's friend and fellow-philanthropist, an honorable man who had achieved a distinguished reputation as a Fellow of the Royal Society and of the Society of Antiquaries, as shipping tycoon, and as Chairman of Lloyd's Register of Shipping. Not least for Powell, Chapman had forgiven him his trespasses and enabled him to escape to New York, though he was the chief victim of his nephew.

Dickens was not one to be trifled with, especially when abuse was directed at what he liked to call "the property." As he had told Powell in the good old days, "It will take a long time to do, but vengeance is strong, and Dickens persevering." The novelist thus proceeded to expose Powell's criminal record in

England and America, an exposure that was as widely published as had been Powell's abuse of him.

This exchange launched a vendetta that caught international attention and finally led Powell to bring libel suits against those editors who had published Dickens's exposure. One of his lawsuits was against Dickens himself. From this decade-long episode, the novelist's ideas for the Carker brothers (*Dombey and Son*), Uriah Heep (*David Copperfield*), and Jarndyce and Jarndyce (*Bleak House*) derived in large part.

This story is told here with all its pertinent retrievable pieces collected and in place for the first time. The documents, together with the headnotes, are designed to give the reader a sense of being an eyewitness to the events as they suspensefully unfold.

THE BACKGROUND OF THE VENDETTA

"When we doos go in, we plays to win."
—Charles Dickens to Thomas Powell

1. *5 March 1844: Excerpt from "Charles Dickens" in* A New Spirit of the Age

Thomas Powell and R. H. Horne

In 1843 R. H. Horne, poet and journalist, began to edit a collection of essays whose contributors were to include Elizabeth Barrett, Leigh Hunt (who declined), and one Thomas Powell, who underwrote the cost of the book. The collection was to be titled, A New Spirit of the Age*—to update, as it were, Hazlitt's* The Spirit of the Age, *published twenty years earlier.*

The place of honor in the two-volume work was awarded to Dickens, though the collection featured, among others, Landor, Wordsworth, Tennyson, Macaulay, Martineau, Browning, Bulwer, and Carlyle. (Two pirated one-volume versions of the work were published in New York, also in 1844.)

The question arises, Who wrote the essay on Dickens? The answer is not as forthcoming as one would wish. Contributors to the collection were anonymous and honor-bound to keep their authorship secret. When a leak occurred, for example, Elizabeth Barrett "solemnly assure[d]" Horne that she had "never mentioned the subject" of her involvement in A New Spirit *"even to my own father" (Mayer, 1:168). Thomas Powell, in notes found in his presentation copy to Evert A. Duyckinck (now in the New York Public Library), claimed to have had a large share in the collection, even in its conception. He also "claimed to have written the essay on Dickens jointly with Horne" (P, 3:598n).*

For his part, Horne declared that the "article upon Charles Dickens was written entirely by myself" (Mayer, 1:241). Horne made that declaration in extended notes (to be found in Mayer's edition of Elizabeth Barrett's letters), a declaration suspect for his suppression of any mention of Powell. He even suppressed any mention of Powell in discussing The Poems of Chaucer, Modernized *(ibid.), though Powell undeniably contributed to the volume. Powell was not far from the mark when he wrote some years later: Horne's "chief enemy is a tremendous self-will, which leads him to consider ten thousand acts of kindness cancelled, should any word or deed come to light derogatory to his self-importance" (*Living Authors of England, *221).*

Be that as it may, passing remarks in two Dickens letters gainsay Horne's claim to total authorship of the Dickens essay and support Powell's claim to collaboration, inasmuch as those letters indicate that Horne and Powell were blaming each other for any untoward passages in the essay. On 9 October 1843 Dickens wrote to Powell: "I shall not fail to keep a sharp eye on Horne. Let him beware! If he gives me the least offence, I will unsay all I have said, everywhere, in praise of his report on youthful labour [in the section of The Second Report of the Children's Employment Commission *titled, "The Moral Condition of the whole youthful population"]. It will take a long time to do, but vengeance is strong, and Dickens persevering" (P, 3:578-79 & 459n). When Horne sent a draft or proof of the essay to Dickens the following month, he must have told him that Powell was his collaborator. For when Dickens found two references objectionable (the first to his opera* The Village Coquettes, *the other to his farce, the* "Great Winglebury Duel"*), he urged Horne to "Pray tell that besotted ______ to let the opera sink into its native obscurity . . . and impress . . . on [his] waxy mind" to let the farce be forgotten (P, 3:598). (Powell's name had been blanked out by Georgina Hogarth and Kate Perugini, the original co-editors of the now-vanished letter, if only because Powell was still alive and active.) It would appear, then, that Powell was not only co-author of the essay, but even the dominant author, for Dickens's objections notwithstanding, the references to his two early works remained in the published version. Furthermore, Horne told Elizabeth Barrett that the "puzzles" and errors in the page proof were not his: "I have just read over the Dickens proof, and am vexed you sh'd have seen it in so imperfect a state of revision. You must have had many puzzles—such as Dickens' style being called 'severe'—to say nothing of grammatical slips, several of which, I dare say, are not attributable to the printer" (Kelley & Hudson, 8:195-96). Moreover, Dickens himself was convinced that Powell had had a hand in the authorship of the essay as he continually teased the man about making him a spirit—a take-off on* A Spirit of the Age *(Documents 4 & 5).*

Apart from those two references, nothing seems to have troubled Dickens about the essay, as its seventy-five pages were as laudatory as he might wish. Nor was he troubled when a second edition of A New Spirit *appeared in August to drop the collection and its editor deeper into critical contempt (Blainey, 144-46), what with its added dead weight of thirty pages of defensive commentary which took on such critics as Thackeray for "unscrupulous hilarity" in his review of the original edition. Indeed, the only thing that troubled Dickens was the frontispiece, which made him, he said, "look a leetle like the man in the iron mask." However, another essay on Dickens, indisputably written by Powell alone and published five years later, would trouble him humongously and initiate a vendetta.*

. . . There are no caricatures in the portraits of Hogarth, nor are there any in those of Dickens. The most striking thing in both is their apparently inexhaustible variety and truth of character. . . . How very like they [Hogarth's portraits] are to many scenes in the works of Dickens . . . in moral purpose and finished execution of parts. . . .

But the comic humour for which these two great masters of character are most popularly known, constitutes a part only of their genius, and certainly not the highest part. Both possess tragic power—not at all in the ideal world, nor yet to be regarded as mere harsh, unredeemed matter-of-fact reality—but of the profoundest order. Mingled with their graphic tendencies to portray absurdity and ugliness, both display a love for the beautiful, and the pathetic. In the latter respect more especially, Mr. Dickens greatly excels; and two or three of his scenes, and numerous incidental touches, have never been surpassed if the heart-felt tears of tens of thousands of readers are any test of natural pathos. But although their tragic power is so great, it is curious to observe that neither Hogarth nor Dickens has ever portrayed a tragic character, in the higher or more essential sense of the term. . . . In their works no one dies for a noble purpose, nor for an abstract passion. There is no walking to execution, or to a premature grave by any other means, with a lofty air of conscious right, and for some great soul-felt truth—no apprehension for a capital crime in which there is a noble bearing or exultation—no death-bed of greatness in resignation and contentment for the cause—for there is no great cause at stake. Their tragedy is the constant tragedy of private life—especially with the poorer classes. They choose a man or woman for this purpose, with sufficient strength of body and will, and for the most part vicious and depraved; they place them in just the right sort of desperate circumstances which will ripen their previous character to its disastrous end; and they then leave the practical forces of nature and society to finish the story. Most truly, and fearfully, and morally, is it all done—or rather, it all seems to happen, and we read it as a fac-simile, or a most faithful chronicle. Their heroes are without any tragic principle or purpose in themselves: they never tempt their fate or run upon destruction, but rush away from it, evade, dodge, hide, fight, wrestle, tear and scream at it as a downright horror, and finally die because they absolutely cannot help it. This is shown or implied in most of the violent deaths which occur in the works of these two inventive geniuses.

. . . In dealing with repulsive characters and actions, the former sometimes does so in a repulsive manner, not artistically justifiable by any means, because it is a gross copy of the fact. The latter, never does this; and his power of dealing with the worst possible characters, at their worst moments, and suggesting their worst language, yet never once committing himself, his book, or his reader, by any gross expression or unredeemed action, is one of the most marvelous examples of fine skill and good taste the world ever saw, and one great (negative) cause of his universal popularity. . . .

Mr. Dickens is one of those happily constituted individuals who can "touch pitch without soiling his fingers"; the peculiar rarity, in his case, being that he can do so without gloves; and, grasping its clinging blackness with both hands, shall yet retain no soil, nor ugly memory. . . . In "Oliver Twist"—the work which is most full of crimes and atrocities and the lowest characters, of all its author's productions, in which these things are by no means scarce—there are some of the deepest touches of pathos, and of the purest tenderness, not exceeded by any author who ever lived—simply because they grow out of the very ground of our common humanity, and being Nature at her best, are in themselves perfect, by universal laws. Of this kind is the scene where the poor sweet-hearted consumptive child, who is weeding the garden before anybody else has risen, climbs up the gate, and puts his little arms through to clasp Oliver round the neck, and kiss him "a good bye," as he is running away from his wretched apprenticeship. . . . O, ye scions of a refined age—readers of the scrupulous taste, who, here and there, in apprehensive circles, exclaim upon Dickens as a low writer, and a lover of low scenes—look at this passage—find out *how* low it is—and rise up from the contemplation chastened, purified—wiser, because sorrow-softened and better men through the enlargement of sympathies. . . .

Both [Hogarth and Dickens] have been accused of a predilection for the lower classes of society, from inability to portray those of the upper classes. Now, the predilection being admitted, the reason of this is chiefly attributable to the fact that there is little if any humour or genuine wit in the upper classes, where all *gusto* of that kind is polished away; and also to the fact that both of them have a direct moral purpose in view, viz., a desire to ameliorate the condition of the poorer classes by showing what society has made of them, or allowed them to become—and to continue. . . .

That Mr. Dickens often caricatures, has been said by many people; but if they examined their own minds they would be very likely to find that this opinion chiefly originated, and was supported by certain undoubted caricatures among the illustrations. *Le célèbre Cruikshank*—as the French translator of "Nicholas Nickleby" calls him, appears sometimes to have made his sketches without due reference, if any, to the original. These remarks, however, are far from being intended to invalidate the great excellence of many of the illustrations in "Oliver Twist" and "Nicholas Nickleby," and also of those by Hablot Browne and Cattermole in "Barnaby Rudge" and "Martin Chuzzlewit."

What a collection—what a motley rout—what a crowd—what a conflict for precedence in the mind, as we pause to contemplate these beings with whom Mr. Dickens has over-peopled our literature. Yet there are but few which, all things considered, we should wish to "emigrate". . . .

In his young lady heroines Mr. Dickens is not equally successful. They have a strong tendency to be unromantically dutiful, which in real life, is no doubt "an excellent thing in woman," but it is apt, unless founded upon some truly noble principle, to become uninteresting in fiction. Their sacrifices to duty are generally common-place, conventional, and of very equivocal good, if not quite erroneous. Some of the amiable old gentlemen are also of the description so very agreeable to meet in private life, but who do not greatly advantage the interests of these books, amidst the raciness and vigour of which they hardly form the right sort of contrast. With reference to his female characters, however, who are "better-halves," if his portraits be faithful representations, especially of the middle and lower classes,—and it is greatly to be feared they are but *too* true, in many cases—then we shall discover the alarming amount of screws, scolds, tartars, and termagants, over whom her Britannic Majesty's liege married subjects male, pleasantly assume to be "lords and masters." France lifts its shoulders at it, and Germany turns pale. . . .

Certainly not the highest, but certainly the most prominent characteristic of Mr. Dickens' mind, is his humour. His works furnish a constant commentary on the distinction between wit and humour; for of sheer wit, either in remark or repartee, there is scarcely an instance in any of his volumes, while of humour there is a fullness and *gusto* in every page, which would be searched for in vain to such an extent, among all other authors. It is not meant that there are not several authors, and of the present time, who might equal the best points of humour in any of Mr. Dickens' works, but there is no author who can "keep it up" as he does; no author who can fill page after page with unfailing and irresistible humour, the only "relief" to which, if any, shall be fun, and the exuberance of animal spirits. . . .

But if Mr. Dickens does not display anything of what is recognized as sheer wit in his writings, he frequently indulges in irony, and sometimes in sarcasm. To his great credit, these instances are never of a morbid misanthropical kind, and in the shape of trenchant side hits and stabs at human nature; they will almost invariably be found directed against social wrongs, "the insolence of office," against false notions of honour, against mere external respectability, and with a view to defend the poor against injustice and oppression. . . .

Our author is conspicuous for his graphic powers. All his descriptions are good, often excellent; sometimes, both for minute truths and general effect, perfect. Humorous descriptions are his forte; and serious description is no less his forte, though he far less often indulges in it. Perhaps it may be said that his *eye* is "worth all his other senses"; at all events, it is never "made the fool" of the other senses—except where it ought to be so (sympathetically) in describing objects seen through the medium of passion. It will presently be shown that this exception constitutes one of the finest elements, if not the finest element of his genius. But the feature in his writings, now under consideration, is the power he possesses of describing things as they actually exist. . . .

A pure feeling of religion, and a noble spirit of Christian charity and active benevolence is apparent in all appropriate places throughout the works of Charles Dickens. . . .

Mr. Dickens is manifestly the product of his age. He is a genuine emanation from its aggregate and entire spirit. He is not an imitator of any one. He mixes extensively in society, and continually. Few public meetings in a benevolent cause are without him. He speaks effectively—humorously, at first, and then seriously to the point. His reputation, and all the works we have discussed, are the extraordinary product of only eight years. Popularity and success, which injure so many men in head and heart, have improved him in all respects. His influence upon his age is extensive—pleasurable, instructive, healthy, reformatory. If his "Christmas Carol" were printed in letters of gold, there would be no inscriptions which would give a more salutary hint to the gold of a country. As for posterity, let no living man pronounce upon it; but if an opinion may be offered, it would be that the earlier works of Mr. Dickens—the "Sketches by Boz," and some others—will die natural deaths; but that his best productions, such as "Nicholas Nickleby," the "Old Curiosity Shop," "Oliver Twist," and "Martin Chuzzlewit," will live as long as our literature endures, and take rank with the works of Cervantes, of Hogarth, and De Foe.

Mr. Dickens is, in private, very much what might be expected from his works,—by no means an invariable coincidence. He talks much or little according to his sympathies. His conversation is genial. He hates argument; in fact, he is unable to argue—a common case with impulsive characters who see the whole truth, and feel it crowding and struggling at once for immediate utterance. He never talks for effect, but for the truth or for the fun of the thing. He tells a story admirably, and generally with humorous exaggerations. His sympathies are of the broadest, and his literary tastes appreciate all excellence. He is a great admirer of the poetry of Tennyson. Mr. Dickens has singular personal activity, and is fond of games of practical skill. He is also a great walker, and very much given to dancing Sir Roger de Coverley. In private, the general impression of him is that of a first-rate practical intellect, with "no nonsense" about him. Seldom, if ever, has any man been more beloved by contemporary authors, and by the public of his time. . . .

---

2. *9 October 1843: From a Letter to Thomas Powell*

Charles Dickens

*Thomas Powell (1809-87), the office manager and head accountant in the firm of John Chapman & Co., was described, even in his old age, as a "bluff Englishman, large, beef-eating, and giving out the promise of good living" (*New York Mirror*, 19 Jan. 1887). In his youth, Powell tells us, he had been taken into the London firm of John Chapman & Co. by his uncle Thomas Chapman at No. 2 Leadenhall Street in the City ("Leaves from My Life," 135). Though no genius himself, he had a genius for cultivating friendships with the literary genius of the age: among them, Wordsworth, Lamb, Southey, Landor, Hunt, Browning, and Elizabeth Barrett. A lavish entertainer, he courted them with "sumptuous banquets" (Document 58) and "edible presents" of kippered salmon, pressed tongues, jellies, and pickles (Blainey, 114); or, as Dickens put it on one occasion, by "elegant present[s]," such as the "1st Ed: of the Paradise Lost" he gave to Wordsworth (Hill, 298), his "very dear friend," to cite Barrett. Add to his generous and genial nature the fact that he was a wit, a raconteur, and a bon vivant, and it is easy to see why he was taken up by so many gifted individuals.*

When Powell met Dickens in 1842 (they were both in their early thirties), he had published a number of articles, some unstaged verse plays, and a book of poems. In concert with such friends as Wordsworth, Leigh Hunt, R. H. Horne, and Elizabeth Barrett, Powell had also projected, contributed to, and promoted Chaucer's Poems, Modernized *(1841); and, as with* A New Spirit of the Age, *he graciously permitted Horne to assume the editorship of that work. The projected second volume of* Chaucer, *for which the services of Tennyson, Bulwer, Browning, and Talfourd were to be sought, never materialized, for the reviews, on the whole, were devastating.* The Athenaeum *(6 Feb. 1841), for instance, condemned Horne for diluting Chaucer "to the level of cockney comprehensions."*

The way that Powell courted Dickens is indicated below.

Top: **Ad in *The Athenaeum.***

Dr. Leonhard Schmitz, classicist and historian, was the husband of the sister of Thomas Powell's wife, née Frances Maria Machell. A naturalized British subject, he was much honored for his achievements, but the professorship was awarded him only by Powell.

Bottom: **Ad in *The Athenaeum.***

Charles Dickens c. 1850 at about age 38
From the original by Henri Claudet
Taken during the time of Dickens's vendetta with Thomas Powell
By permission of Huntington Library

Thomas Powell c. age 77
The man who began the vendetta
(No earlier image of Powell seems to exist)
From *Frank Leslie's Illustrated Newspaper* (1887)

Thomas Chapman c. age 78
The man whom Powell accused Dickens of
"grossly libelling and caricaturing" as Paul Dombey
(No earlier image of Chapman seems to exist)
By permission of Lloyd's of London

My Dear Sir

Mrs. Dickens is much beholden to you for your kind recollection of her, and for your elegant present. She begs me to thank you most cordially. I should have done so, before now; but we have been out of town, and I returned only yesterday.

---

3. *8 February 1844: From a Letter to Thomas Chapman*

Charles Dickens

The man under whom Thomas Powell worked was Thomas Chapman (1798-1885), the senior proprietor of John Chapman & Co., a firm founded by his great-uncle, a shipowner from Whitby, who was the father of his inactive partner, Aaron Chapman, a Member of Parliament, also from Whitby. Thomas Chapman was "nurtured in the lap of wealth . . . and received a superior education, though intended for mercantile pursuits" (Browne, 106). That he was successful in those pursuits is beyond question. For one thing, he became a tycoon in the shipping business. "The House," as Dickens liked to designate Chapman & Co., was in the export/import business, with employees stationed at key points in England's colonial empire to arrange for the collection and shipping of merchandise. The House also had the capability of leasing ships from its merchant fleet.

For another thing, given his wealth, eminence, and intelligence, to say nothing of his "consummate tact, urbanity of manner and conciliatory disposition" (Browne, 110), Chapman at age thirty-seven was elected the Chairman of Lloyd's Register of British and Foreign Shipping (unconnected with Lloyds of London since 1760), a position he held uninterruptedly until 1881. Little wonder that he came to be known as the "Father of Lloyd's Register," especially when, one Christmas season when times were tough, he paid salaries out of his own pocket (Blake, 55).

The importance of Lloyd's Register can hardly be exaggerated. Begun as a society composed of merchants, underwriters, and shipholders of London, it became a world-famous corporation which included shipbuilders, engineers, steelmakers, and representatives from other parts of the United Kingdom and thirteen maritime countries who set standards for the construction and maintenance of ships throughout the world. Lloyd's Register of Shipping *and its supplements give, among a wealth of other information, the latest intelligence concerning names, classes, ownership, flag, tonnage, etc., of merchant ships. Given his position, Chapman became a major underwriter at Lloyds (Blake, 22). Later in life he became a director of the London and Westminster Bank and of the Atlas Assurance Company (Browne, 111).*

As might be expected, honors were heaped upon Chapman. He was made a Fellow of the Royal Society, a Fellow of the Society of Antiquaries, and Vice-President of the Institute of Naval Architects, to name the more distinguished ones.

Dickens, who tended to gravitate to the rich and powerful, was pleased to claim Chapman as friend. To Miss Burdett Coutts, the wealthiest woman in England, whom he also claimed as friend, he wrote: "My own personal friend Mr. Chapman, is the Chairman of the shipping Committee of Lloyds; and the House are merchants, and large ship-owners." Dickens added that he had first met Chapman "in connexion with the Sanitorium," of which Prince Albert was President, Chapman Chairman, and himself a Director (P, 5:435 & 3:384n). Their friendship was such that they and their wives dined at each other's house on occasion (P, 4:133 & 6:686).

When Dickens's youngest brother Augustus had finished school and was at loose ends, Dickens bethought of his friendship with Chapman and wrote him the letter that appears below. (Augustus's life is recorded in Moss & Moss.)

My Dear Sir

Pray excuse my troubling you with a petition. But my City friends are not numerous; and casting about how to strive after an object I have very much at heart just now, it occurred to me as just coming within the bounds of possibility that you might be able to assist me.

I have a young brother (about Seventeen) recently come up from a good school at Exeter, and now living, with his father, at Greenwich. I am extremely anxious to get employment for him in the office of some respectable house, where he would carry (in his pockets) such metal as is usually bestowed on such small craft. He is quick, and clever; has never given any trouble to anybody; and has been well brought up. Above all, I have no reason to suppose that he is addicted to authorship, or any bad habits of that nature.

If any such thing should present itself before you at any time, and you will kindly think of the Committee-man who never comes to the Sanitorium (in consequence, chiefly, of living close to it: which is a terrible drawback) you will confer a very great obligation on him.

I beg my compliments to Mrs. Chapman. To whom I am happy to report that Mrs. Dickens is doing extremely well [in recovering from childbirth].

My Dear Sir/Faithfully Yours/Charles Dickens

---

4. *24 February 1844: From a Letter to Thomas Powell*

Charles Dickens

In response to Dickens's letter (Document 3), Thomas Chapman arranged to have Augustus Dickens interviewed by Powell, his head accountant and office manager, with an eye to Augustus's serving in Powell's department. (The position of accountant had been dignified somewhat by the well-known fact that Charles Lamb had clerked for thirty-three years in the Accountants' Office of the East India House, which was also located in Leadenhall Street.) To lighten the interview somewhat for his anxious seventeen-year-old brother, Dickens gave him a letter to present to Powell.

"Spirit" is a reference to A New Spirit of the Age, *with which Powell had been involved (Document 1).*

My Dear Powell.

I enclose the brother, concerning whom Mr. Chapman has been so kind as to talk with you. I need not commend him I know (being a Spirit, and I hope a good one) to your favorable regard.

Faithfully Yours Always/Charles Dickens

---

5. *2 March 1884: From a Letter to Thomas Powell*

Charles Dickens

Powell having hired Augustus, Dickens expresses his gratitude to him, even to inviting him to his house at Devonshire Terrace.

Dickens's reference to "Spirit Number one" is to himself, as he was given the place of honor in A New Spirit of the Age.

My Dear Powell.

I really am more indebted and obliged to you than I can express, for your great interest and kindness in the matter of my small "bit of blood"—to use a sporting phrase.

Audiences of twos of thousands have been driving me mad at Liverpool and Birmingham, with their loving cheers [at my readings]. Ah! It is a brave thing, by Heaven it is, to walk out . . . into a sea of agitated faces, and think that they are always looking on—

Woa, Spirit Number one. Woho my boy. Gently, gently. Don't be maudlin, Spirit. Think of your ethereal essence, my buck. Steady, steady.

Come and take a little Ambrosia here, next Sunday (I mean tomorrow week) at 6 exactly, will you? I have a trifle of bottled Dawn—the old Aurora particular—the real crusted Rosy—if you can make your dinner off that, and a Zephyr or two. I shall be delighted to see you.

Ever Faithfully Yours./Ariel.

---

6. *16 April 1844: From a Letter to Thomas Powell*

Charles Dickens

By this time Dickens and Powell have become quite easy with each other, to the point that Dickens draws for him, in Pickwickian fashion, an imaginary dinner party for Thomas Chapman; and, driven by fish imagery, he feels free to call Powell "Prawn" and to sign himself familiarly CD.

"Potted char" is one of the edible presents Powell has given the Dickenses.

My Dear Powell.

Lord bless you! Thursday or Friday!!! Why, I composed (though I say it, as shouldn't) the best little party you can imagine; comprehending everybody I had room for, whom I thought Mr. Chapman would like to know. Let me see. Rogers for Poetry, Sydney Smith for Orthodoxy, Charles Kemble and Young for Theatricality, Lord Denman for Benchity, Lord Dudley Stuart for Polarity, Mr. and Mrs. Milner Gibson for Anti Corn Law Leaguality, Mrs. Norton for beauty, and divers others for variety. Lord love you! Why, at this time of the year it couldn't be done again under three weeks. Not to mention the Dwarf—General Tom Thumb—whom on the word of a Spiritiwal creetur, I had summoned, and have summoned, for the Evening in question. No. We won't come down with the run. We'll have a long notice, and see what can be done with the second wentur. When we doos go in, we plays to win Sir.

Says Shrimp to me (I allude to the humble individual who has the honor to be my brother) "Mr. Powell is coming up one evening".—"Shrimp", said I. "Why evening? We dine at half past 5. Cannot said Powell, with a day's notice (to ensure my not being out) come up to dinner?" I saw that I had touched him; and had a modest confidence in my Message reaching you safely. Whether Shrimp broke down, or Prawn (otherwise Powell) I don't know. But until this point is cleared up, I decline to acknowledge the receipt of potted chair [char]. If indeed that *be* chair in a black bag; which I don't believe.

Faithfully Ever/CD.

---

7. *2 August 1845: From a Letter to Thomas Powell*

Charles Dickens

An unidentified "young Lady" in Chapman's employ and Dickens's now eighteen-year-old brother Augustus are having an office romance. Fearing that the girl may have ulterior designs upon Augustus, Powell notifies Dickens of the romance, and Dickens pens a reply.

My Dear Powell.

I intend handing this to Augustus (whom I expect so see here, tomorrow) to bring to you. But he is quite innocent of its subject or contents.

I have thought several times of what you said to me in Broad Street, and am disposed (subject always to your corrective judgment) to leave the matter where it is. I will tell you why.

In the first place, I think any grave notice of such a thing to a youth of Augustus's years, very likely to invest it with an importance not otherwise attaching to it in his eyes. In the second, I am relieved from any oppressive anxiety touching the young Lady's designs upon him, by the knowledge that he has no possessions of any sort or kind. In the third, I contemplate the great possibility of there being nothing at all in it, but a means of getting rid of spare time pleasantly. In the fourth, and at the worst, I am not at all sure but it may keep him out of other harm's way.

I broke my heart into the smallest pieces, many times between thirteen and three and twenty. Twice, I was very horribly in earnest; and once I really set upon the cast for six or seven long years, all the energy and determination of which I am owner. But it went the way of nearly all such things at last, though I think it kept me steadier than the working of my nature was, to many good things for the time. If anyone had interfered with my very small Cupid, I don't know what absurdity I might not have committed in assertion of his proper liberty; but having plenty of rope he hanged himself, beyond all chance of restoration.

I have asked no questions of my father or mother, for though I am dutiful, I am not altogether disposed to trust to their discretion in such a case. But I have sounded my brother Fred; and he seems to think the Virgin may be "only joking". She may be a Platonic Virgin, perhaps. Who knows!

In any case, without further communication with you, I am unwilling to seem to recognize the possibility of there being any danger either of contract or contact between Augustus and the Damsel. And this is not a hasty opinion, I assure you.

Now, what do *you* say?

Ever Yours Faithfully/Charles Dickens

---

8. *20 February 1846: From a Letter to Thomas Powell*

Charles Dickens

At Powell's request, Dickens attempted, without success, to place his friend's epigrams with the Daily News, *though John Forster, Dickens's closest friend, business agent, and even proofreader, was now editor of that paper, having succeeded Dickens in that position eleven days earlier.*

My Dear Powell.

I sent your Epigrams, forthwith, to the working Editor of the D.N. I fear, however, that they may be considered too personal for that Immaculate Newspaper.

Faithfully Yours/Charles Dickens

---

9. *19 May 1846: From a Letter to Thomas Powell*

Charles Dickens

On 31 May 1846 the Charles Dickens family left for the continent, to settle in Switzerland after some touring, and would not return to Devonshire Terrace until 25 June 1847. Powell, being in the shipping business, had arranged to ship Dickens's crate to Switzerland.

Unmistakably, Dickens and Powell have become good friends.

My Dear Powell.

I am very much obliged to you for the trouble you have taken about my Box. Is there anything I can do for you in Switzerland—any apple or other fruit I can shoot off any friend's or relation's head—in return? . . . .

Faithfully Yours/Charles Dickens

---

10. *3 July 1846: From a Letter to Thomas Chapman*

Charles Dickens

This letter to Chapman is in response to one that Dickens received from him some time before he began Dombey and Son. *In it Chapman had informed Dickens that Thomas Powell was found to have defrauded John Chapman & Co. of some £10,000—a great sum by Victorian standards, but not so great by Chapman's. He dismissed Powell but did not have him prosecuted, a charitableness he may have exercised for the sake of Powell's family and for the fact that Powell was his nephew, but just as likely to let the scandal pass quietly. (That Chapman was Powell's uncle was a secret so well kept that neither Augustus nor Charles Dickens had an inkling of it, though Powell dropped teasing hints from time to time. Powell "always hinted at a Rich Uncle," as Dickens noted in the letter below. In 1886—a year after Chapman's death and a year before his own agonizing demise when he had no reason to deceive—Powell in "Leaves from My Life" again alluded to Chapman when he spoke of his "uncle's place of business in Leadenhall Street." Unfortunately, definitive confirmation of this connection cannot be made, for while Powell's death certificate names Thomas Powell" as his father, it fails to name his mother. She might have been Chapman's sister or, as seems likelier, the sister of Maria Louisa Hanson, Chapman's wife, which would have made Chapman Powell's uncle by marriage.) Since* The Times, *let alone other papers, regularly reported court news, legal proceedings might well have caused a sensation and shaken confidence in the House. Moreover, according to Dickens, another reason for Powell's not being prosecuted was that, when exposed as a thief, he attempted suicide. He had overdosed on laudanum and was found insensible in a warm bath (Document 28).*

Chapman reported Powell's defalcations to Dickens, as Dickens would no doubt have heard the story from Augustus anyway. Indeed, Chapman probably asked Augustus for his brother's address, as Dickens was then living in Switzerland.

In his reply to Chapman, Dickens's sympathies were all with Powell, they had become such fast friends. On Christmas Day 1845 and again in January 1846, for instance, Dickens had booked "the best boxes" for "friends of mine . . . Mr. and Mrs. Powell" *(P, 4:454-55, 482). He spoke of Powell's being "overcome and swept away by the tide of circumstances on which he had madly cast himself. The more I see and hear of such surprises, the more I echo that clause ["lead us not into temptation"] in Christ's prayer in which they are all shadowed forth,—and shrink from the prospect of temptation being presented to anybody dear to me, or to myself." Even when Dickens decided to feature Powell as John Carker in* Dombey, *he showed sympathy for him (Document 14). Yet here in this letter, after three years of friendship, he pretends to have no "intimate knowledge of his pursuits, or any close acquaintance with himself or his usual mode of thinking and proceeding." Rather inconsistently, however, he avers in the same letter: "I could hardly name a man in London whom I should have thought less likely to stand so committed. . . . I had an idea of his great steadiness and reliability."*

Steadiness and reliability: a curious characterization, considering Powell's reputation in literary circles. For as early as 21 June 1843, Vincent Leigh Hunt was suggesting the shadiness of Powell's character to his mother: "The thing that would do him [Powell] most good would be a year's imprisonment for debt, and a week's starvation:—but in the meantime it is hard indeed that the best of us should suffer for his over-easy condition. He can shed tears over the story of Ugolino but appears deaf to the sufferings of his friend [Leigh Hunt], and one whom he calls his father*" (Munby, 26).*

*Also, no doubt on the word of Horne, Browning told Elizabeth Barrett (12 January 1846) that Ugolino was Hunt's work, which Powell had passed off as his own. "I did not think," Browning added, that Powell was a "*buyer *of other men's verses, to be printed as his own; thus he* bought *two modernisations of Chaucer—'Ugolino' and another story from Leigh Hunt—and one, 'Sir Thopas' from Horne, and printed them as his own, as I learned only last week" (Browning,* fils, *1:391). Moreover, as it became clear enough from his fraudulence at Chapman's, Powell could forge signatures. Browning referred to a volume "containing the autographs—all forged—of Browning, Wordsworth, and Leigh Hunt" (Hood, 374). And the poet added: he "actually practised forging on every possible occasion,—would send you, for instance, a letter signed 'Dickens' or 'Thackeray'" (ibid., 262). Was it Dickens or Powell himself who presented to Powell's eldest boy a "copy of the original London edition of the 'Christmas Carol' . . . [with] the entire inside of the* *first-cover page . . . occupied with a kind and genial notelet addressed to the lad and signed Charles Dickens"? (Document 71, "The Original Micawber").*

*If Powell's notoriety escaped Dickens, though literary gossip was rife in his circle, he must have known, to quote Elizabeth Barrett's remarks to Horne (16-17 June 1844): "Mr Powell passes for having the whole of his hand in the work [*A New Spirit of the Age*] . . . & indeed once somebody told me, that . . . Mr. Horne cd. not help himself," as Powell was one of the proprietors of the collection. (In his* Living Authors of England*, 222, Powell refers to himself as* the *"proprietor of the work.") And Dickens must also have heard Horne's dubious protest that Powell "did* not *write one line in the book" (Kelley & Lewis, 9:18, 19). After all, Dickens knew Horne as well as he knew Powell and must have been distrustful of their mutually contradictory claims and suspicious, in consequence, of their veracity, not to speak of their "steadiness and reliability." Indeed, the Horne-Powell feud was such that Horne in* A New Spirit of the Age *(2:167-68) arbitrarily interpolated at the last minute and without any relevance at all a disparagement of Powell's plays and his poems (ibid., 173-74). Powell would repay Horne with the same coin when he published his essay on Horne in* Living Authors of England *(210-25).*

My Dear Sir

It was a very considerate and friendly act of you to time your communication on the most painful subject of the breach of confidence in your house, as you did, and to make it to me yourself. Accept my thanks for this proof of your regard among many others: and with them the assurance of my friendship and esteem.

I have been perfectly horrified by the whole Story. I could hardly name a man in London whom I should have thought less likely to stand so committed, than he. Not that I had any intimate knowledge of his pursuits, or any close acquaintance with himself or his usual mode of thinking and proceeding—but I had an idea of his great steadiness and reliability, and a conviction of his great respect and regard for you. God help him, I believe, even now, that he was sincere in the latter feeling, and was overcome and swept away by the tide of circumstances on which he had madly cast himself. The more I see and hear of such surprises, the more I echo that clause in Christ's prayer in which they are all shadowed forth,—and shrink from the prospect of temptation being presented to anybody dear to me, or to myself.

It has often awakened great wonder within me how all those publishing expenses (of the extent of which, I was able to form a pretty accurate idea) were defrayed. But whenever I have sounded Augustus on the subject; which I have done once or twice; he always hinted at a Rich Uncle, and some unknown share in some unknown business, which of course I could not gainsay. He told the tale as it was told to him, and had every reason to believe it. Indeed, I suppose you and your partners laboured under the like delusion?

I should be very glad if you would tell me, when it is all done, whether you have any intelligence of him, or any knowledge of his destiny. It is terrible to think of his wife and children. . . .

I have hardly left myself room to say . . . always My Dear Mr. Chapman

Faithfully Your friend/Charles Dickens

---

11. *3 December 1883: From a Letter to Dr. Frederick James Furnivall*

Robert Browning

This letter, taken out of chronological sequence, reflects further on Thomas Powell's notoriety.

Dr. Furnivall founded the Browning Society in 1881, one of many that he inaugurated: the Early English Texts Society, the Chaucer Society, the Ballad Society, the New Shakespere Society, the Shelley Society, and the Wyclif Society.

In answer to Furnivall's query about Thomas Powell, Browning sent him the letter below (Hood, 225). He had little reason to feel kindly toward Powell, for the man had borrowed his "rare first edition of Adonais, *published at Pisa, and sold it" (Thomas, 262). Powell had also tried to obtain copies of Browning's juvenile poems from the poet's father (ibid.), no doubt to turn a profit with them.*

[Thomas Powell] was a person of infamous character, an unparalleled forger, who only escaped transportation through the ill-deserved kindness of his employers; and who, premeditating a defence of "inborn and ineradicable dishonesty," actually practised forging on every possible occasion. . . . I heard he had libelled me, who found him out earlier than most of his dupes.

---

12. *28 June 1846: From a Charles Dickens Letter*

Quoted by John Forster

Dickens begins a new novel, Dombey and Son, *whose full title,* Dealings with the Firm of Dombey and Son, Wholesale, Retail and for Exportation, *suggests the nature of Chapman & Co.'s business.*

The novel was serialized, with the first number appearing on 1 October 1846, the last on 31 March 1848.

Why, of all names, did Dickens fix on one borne by no one in London, according to Kelly's Post Office London Directory, 1846? *It has no special ring like those of other* Dombey *characters: Cuttle, Gills, Gay, Mac Stinger, and Pipchin, among others.*

One explanation appeared in the New York Mirror *(29 January 1887). According to that newspaper, at the time Dickens was thinking of a title for his projected novel, a firm of London tailors was "plastering the walls of highways and besetting the public on every hand with the eternal iteration of their name—Dowdney & Son. Dickens . . . caught on, and hence 'Dombey & Son' availed itself of the advertising cyclone started up by the ready money of the enterprising tailors" ("The Original Micawber," Document 71).*

The report seems plausible enough, given the fact that Kelly's London Directory *listed a firm of tailors called Edward P. Doudney & Son at 49 Lombardy Street. (Typos—the inadvertent switch of a* w *for a* u *in this instance—were common in nineteenth century newspapers.) Another firm of tailors, the Doudney Brothers, in all likelihood related to Doudney & Son, operated two shops, one at 97 Fleet Street, the other at 17 Old Bond Street.*

BEGAN DOMBEY!

I performed this feat yesterday—only wrote the first slip—but there it is, and it is a plunge straight over head and ears into the story. . . . By the way, as I was unpacking . . . I took hold of a book, and said . . . "Now, whatever passage my thumb rests on, I shall take as having reference to my work." It was Tristram Shandy, and opened at these words, "What a work it is likely to turn out! Let us begin it!"

---

13. *18 July 1846: From a Charles Dickens Letter*

Quoted by John Forster

In the process of writing Chapter 4 of Dombey, *Dickens identifies for Forster the purported* physical *model for Dombey, a name that Forster blanked out and whose initials he may have altered in his* Life of Charles Dickens *(1:399-400), for no one has yet been able to attach anyone of Dickens's acquaintance with "A. E. of D.'s."*

Dickens wanted to be quite certain that Hablôt K. Browne (Phiz), the novel's illustrator, did not delineate Dombey in any way that might resemble Chapman; for, as was often observed when the serial was appearing, "there were readers who were sure they recognized the character as Thomas Chapman, in whose Leadenhall Street business Dickens's young brother Augustus was employed" (Johnson, 596). Browne, for one reason or another, did not trouble to see the mysterious Sir A. E. of D.'s or visit Dickens in Lausanne where he was writing the novel. Instead, Browne sent him a set of pencil drawings (now in the Forster Collection, Victoria & Albert Museum Library), four of which Dickens apparently approved, as they are marked by arrows (Horsman, 866). These preliminary studies of Dombey showing these arrows have been published (Buchanan-Brown, plate 112, and Kitton, Phiz, *10). A similar situation arose when Dickens was satirizing Leigh Hunt as Skimpole in* Bleak House. *He wrote to Forster: "Browne has done Skimpole, and helped to make him singularly unlike the great original": short and fat rather than tall and lean (P, 6:623).*

. . . The points for illustration, and the enormous care required, make me excessively anxious. The man for Dombey, if Browne could see him, the class man to a T, is Sir A_____ E_______, of D_______'s."

Paul Dombey
He Heads the House of Dombey and Son

John Carker
He Figures in "The Brother's Story"

Details from Two Phiz Illustrations in **Dombey and Son**

Dickens wanted Phiz to draw a figure of Dombey that would in no way suggest a resemblance to Thomas Chapman. By the same token, Dickens would not have wanted the figure of John Carker to suggest Thomas Powell; hence these representations.

14. *1 January 1847: Two Passages Relating to the Thomas Powell Story in* **Dombey and Son**

Charles Dickens

Dickens was meditating the plot of Dombey and Son *when he received the news of Powell's defalcations—first from Augustus in all likelihood and then from Thomas Chapman. He decided to use the Powell story by splitting it between two brothers, the tempted but now redeemed John Carker and James Carker, the office manager, who was intent upon bringing Dombey and his House down, with no disadvantage to himself.*

Dickens's projection for Chapter 13 reads in part: "Shipping intelligence and office business/Picture of the Counting house—Introduce/Mr [James] Carker the Manager, and his brother [John Carker]./Brother's story." Dickens's projection for Chapter 53 reads in part: "Mr Morfin/ . . . tells [Harriet Carker] about James Carker, and/shadows forth Mr Dombey's ruin."

The two speeches that appear below indicate how Dickens split the Powell story. The first speech is reminiscent of Powell's depredations upon Chapman & Co. and Chapman's forgiveness of him. The second speech, delivered by Morfin, James Carker's assistant accountant, draws upon Powell's fraudulent manipulation of the ledgers, though Carker's purpose in doing so was hardly Powell's, whose only interest was in maintaining his high style. Incidentally, there were "three heads of the House" of Chapman & Co.—Thomas Chapman, Aaron Chapman, and John Allan.

"It was begun," said Carker, "before my twenty-first birthday—led up to, long before, but not begun till near that time. I had robbed them [the House of Dombey & Son] when I came of age. I robbed them afterwards. Before my twenty-second birthday, it was all found out; and then, Walter, from all men's society, I died. . . .

"The House was very good to me. May Heaven reward the old man [Dombey senior, now dead] for his forbearance! This one, too, his son, who was then newly in the firm, where I had held great trust! I was called into that room which is now his [Dombey's]—I have never entered it since—and came out, what you know me. For many years I sat in my present seat, alone as now, but then a known and recognized example to the rest [of the clerks]. They were all merciful to me, and I lived. Time has altered that part of my poor expiation; and I think, except the three heads of the House, there is no one here who knows my story rightly. Before the little boy [Paul Dombey] grows up, and has it told to him, my corner may be vacant. I would rather that it might be so! This is the only change to me since that day, when I left all youth, and hope, and good men's company, behind me in that room. God bless you, Walter! Keep you, and all dear to you, in honesty, or strike them dead!"

That he has abused his trust in many ways . . .; that he has oftener dealt and speculated to advantage for himself, than for the House he represented; that he has led the House on, to prodigious ventures, often resulting in enormous losses; that he has always pampered the vanity and ambition of his employer, when it was his duty to have held them in check, and shown, as it was in his power to do, to what they tended here or there; will not perhaps surprise you now. Undertakings have been entered on, to swell the reputation of the House for vast resources, and to exhibit it in magnificent contrast to other merchants' houses, of which it requires a steady head to contemplate the possibly—a few disastrous changes of affairs might render them the probably—ruinous consequences. In the midst of the many transactions of the House, in most parts of the world: a great labyrinth of which only he has held the clue: he has had the opportunity, and he seems to have used it, of keeping the various results afloat, when ascertained, and substituting estimates and generalities for facts. . . .

Latterly, he appears to have devoted the greatest pains to making these results so plain and clear, that reference to the private books enables one to grasp them, numerous and varying as they are, with extraordinary ease. As if he had resolved to show his employer at one broad view what has been brought upon him by ministration to his ruling passion! That it has been his constant practice to minister to that passion basely, and to flatter it corruptly, is indubitable. In that, his criminality, as it is connected with the affairs of the House, chiefly consists.

---

15. *22 November 1848: From a Letter to Thomas Chapman*

Charles Dickens

*Dickens invites Chapman to a wedding breakfast for his brother Augustus who, now twenty-one, is to marry Harriette Lovell on 5 December 1848. The invitation makes no mention of Chapman's wife, née Maria Louisa Hanson (*m. *1825;* d. *1877), formerly of Great Bromley Hall in Essex.*

Dickens's letter is so uncharacteristically diffident that one wonders if he had reason to think that Chapman may have seen himself, or some aspects of himself, as Dombey—as Leigh Hunt, for instance, was to see himself as Skimpole in Bleak House. *There were persistent suspicions and rumors that such was indeed the case (Documents 16 & 17). John Forster in his three-volume biography of Dickens (1872-74) denied that Dombey was based on that "excellent city-merchant" (Document 18), who was still quite alive and would remain so until 1885.*

Whether Chapman attended the breakfast for his employee is not known.

Neither Dickens nor Augustus seemed to be aware that at this time Thomas Powell was holed up at the Burgh House near Croydon and supporting himself and his family by forging checks.

My Dear Sir

Mrs. Dickens and I have been often talking of late about one theme. You will be amused when I mention it, I dare say, and will think this an odd sort of beginning. The question has been whether we should ask you to come to breakfast with us in Devonshire Terrace, on the day of Augustus' Marriage.

At last, coming down here [to Brighton] to finish my little Christmas book [*The Haunted Man and the Ghost's Bargain*], I have resolved to write, and using that privilege of friendship which I am sure I *may* use with you, ask you whether I *shall* ask you, or not?

I need not say that I know it would be, in the highest degree, gratifying to Augustus if you were present on an occasion so important to him, and it is as needless for me to add that your coming would give Mrs. Dickens and me a new interest in a little party in which we are almost strangers, as it is mainly composed of his young wife's relations. But I feel it so probable that it might be inconvenient or tiresome to you, or that there may be very rational and necessary considerations to render it "un-business-like" (I use the phrase for want of a better) in reference to so young a man engaged in your house, that I feel the plain course as between you and me is to do just what I do now. Your coming would please me *extremely*, but I should wish it to please you too, and I feel confident that you will use no reserve with me, if I use none on my part.

I cannot let this opportunity pass, without assuring you that I am deeply sensible of your extraordinary kindness to Augustus, and that your interest and your friendly consideration are warmly appreciated by me, and have, from the time of our first communication in reference to him, impressed me in the strongest manner.

Ever My Dear Sir/Very Faithfully Yours/Charles Dickens

---

16. *1870: From* Life of Charles Dickens

R. Shelton Mackenzie, L.L.D.

Mackenzie had a long journalistic career. Irish-born, he served on the staff of several London newspapers and was the first English correspondent for the American press. In 1852 he emigrated to the United States, where he remained until his death in 1880. He has the distinction of publishing the first book-length biography of Dickens; indeed, it appeared in the very year of Dickens's death. At the time, Mackenzie was literary editor of the Philadelphia Press; *hence his dedication of the biography to John W. Forney, his employer.*

Mackenzie's value as a witness is that, directly and indirectly, he was an observer of some of the events involving Dickens. Moreover, as he acknowledged in his Dedication, he drew upon the many personal reminiscences of an "old friend of Mr. Dickens, now resident in New York." That friend was none other than Thomas Powell.

Mackenzie made one error in the excerpt below (201-02): there was not one but two survivors of the "social party" he describes, for Thomas Chapman was also alive at the time and would remain so for fifteen more years.

Mackenzie's description of an area of Leadenhall Street, where the firm of Chapman & Co. was situated, may be compared with Dickens's in Chapter 4 of Dombey *(Document 17). The Wooden Midshipman is now in the Dickens House Museum in London.*

In "*Dombey and Son,*" several characters are said to have been drawn from life. Mr. Dombey is supposed to represent Mr. Thomas Chapman, shipowner, whose offices were opposite the Wooden Midshipman. I had the honor of meeting Mr. Chapman, at dinner, at [John Graham] Lough's, the sculptor, and the rigidity of his manner was only equalled by that of his form; he sat or stood, as the case might be, bolt upright, as if he knew not how to bend—as stiff, in fact, as if he had swallowed the drawing-room poker in his youth, and had never digested it. As if to make Mr. Chapman undoubtedly identical with Dombey, we have, as messenger of the commercial house of "Dombey & Son," one Perch, actually taken from a funny little old chap named Stephen Hale, who was part clerk, part messenger, in Mr. Chapman's office. Old Sol Gills was intended for a little fellow named Norie, who kept a very small shop, in Leadenhall Street exactly opposite the office of John Chapman & Co., in which "the stock in trade comprised chronometers, barometers, telescopes, compasses, charts, maps, sextants, quadrants, and specimens of every kind of instrument used in the working of a ship's course, or the keeping of a ship's reckoning, or the prosecuting of a ship's discoveries."

In front of this small shop stands a figure, carved in wood, and curiously painted, of a miniature midshipman, with a huge quadrant in his hand, as if about taking an observation. What is more, the little shop and the Wooden Midshipman may be seen, by the curious, adorning Leadenhall Street to this very day. I speak of the Wooden Midshipman, as I saw him in 1852. He may have been swept away by what is called "improvement." Captain Cuttle was one David Mainland, master of a merchantman, who was introduced to Dickens on the day when, with Thomas Chapman, Daniel Maclise, John Leech, Thomas Powell, and Samuel Rogers, he went to see Crosby Hall, Bishopgate street, the restoration of which had then (1842) been completed with great taste and skill. This is all that remains of the dwelling of Richard III, repeatedly mentioned by Shakespeare. The bay-window, or oriel, is the *chef d'oeuvre* of the domestic architecture of Old London, and the stone carving is as sharp as when first cut, four centuries ago. The party, my exact informant [Thomas Powell] tells me, proceeded from Crosby Hall to the adjacent London Tavern, also in Bishopgate street, where, at the proper charge of Mr. Thomas Chapman, Bathe & Breach [the proprietors] supplied a lunch. Of the six who constituted that social party, only one survives. On that day, however, Dickens "booked" Captain Cuttle, though he did not appear in *Dombey & Son* until five years later.

---

17. *1 October 1846: From Chapter 4 of* Dombey and Son

Charles Dickens

The description of Dombey's firm and its locale, interesting in its own right as recreating Victorian City life at mid-century, comports well with Mackenzie's recollections in Document 16.

Though the offices of Dombey and Son were within the liberties of the City of London, and within hearing of Bow Bells, when their clashing voices were not drowned by the uproar in the streets, yet were there hints of adventurous and romantic story to be observed in some of the adjacent objects. Gog and Magog held their state within ten minutes' walk; the Royal Exchange was close at hand; the Bank of England with its vaults of gold and silver "down among the dead men" underground, was their magnificent neighbour. Just round the corner stood the rich East India House, teeming with suggestions of precious stuffs and stones, tigers, elephants, howdahs, hookahs, umbrellas, palm trees, palanquins, and gorgeous princes of a brown complexion sitting on carpets with their slippers very much turned up at the toes. Anywhere in the immediate vicinity there might be seen pictures or ships speeding away full sail to all parts of the world; outfitting warehouses ready to pack off anybody anywhere, fully equipped in half an hour; and little timber midshipmen in obsolete naval uniforms, eternally employed outside the shop-doors of nautical instrument makers in taking observations of the hackney coaches.

Sole master and proprietor of one of these effigies—of that which might be called, familiarly, the woodenest—of that which thrust itself out above the pavement, right leg foremost, with a suavity the least endurable, and had the shoe buckles and flapped waistcoat the least reconcileable to human reason, and bore at its right eye the most offensively disproportionate piece of machinery—sole master and proprietor of that Midshipman, and proud of him too, an elderly gentleman in a Welsh wig had paid house-rent, taxes, rates, and dues, for more years than many a full-grown midshipman of flesh and blood has numbered in his life; and midshipmen who have attained a pretty green old age, have not been wanting in the English navy.

The stock-in-trade of this old gentleman comprised chronometers, barometers, telescopes, compasses, charts, maps, sextants, quadrants, and specimens of every kind of instrument used in the working of a ship's course, or the keeping of a ship's reckoning, or the prosecuting of a ship's discoveries.

---

18. *1872-74: Two Passages from* The Life of Charles Dickens

John Forster

Forster was no impartial biographer of Dickens, as he had been the novelist's intimate friend and business and literary adviser. In two separate passages in his biography of Dickens (1:311; 2:35), he denied that Thomas Chapman was the prototype of Paul Dombey, though he reported that Dickens in "reiterated urgent request[s]" made in "several letters . . . expressed his anxiety about the illustrations. A nervous dread of caricature in the face of his merchant-hero, had led him to indicate by a living person the type of city-gentleman he would have had the artist select" (2:23).

The author of The Charles Dickens Originals *(Pugh, 290-91) was amused by Forster's denials. Dickens, he said, was a literary gamester engaged in "high-spirited fun. . . . In urgent need of a nasty stiff proud man . . . [he] hails a friend. 'You, Chapman, be Mr. Dombey. . . .' He is so much like Mr. Dombey that Dickens had considerable trouble with the Phiz pictures; he was so fearful of giving offence to his friend.'"*

With Mr. Thomas Chapman, the chairman of Lloyd's, he held frequent kindly intercourse, and . . . few things more absurd or unfounded have been invented . . . than that he found any part of the original of Mr. Dombey in the nature, the appearance, or the manners of this excellent and much-valued friend.

I think I can say with some confidence . . . that whatever single traits may have been taken from persons known to him (a practice with all writers, and very specially with Dickens), only two had living originals. . . . As to the amiable and excellent city-merchant [Thomas Chapman] whose name has been given to Mr. Dombey, he might with the same amount of justice or probability be supposed to have originated *Coriolanus* or *Timon of Athens*.

---

19. *10 January 1849: "Extraordinary Case"*

The Times

Thomas Powell remained unreformed, despite risking prison, or transportation like Dickens's own Magwitch. Incorrigible, he fell foul of the Croydon police by again forging checks. (Croydon, in Surrey County, was then a market town on the Brighton road, ten miles from London.) Powell had also, according to Browning's letter of 3 December 1848 (Hood, 21), made a "handsome sale of manuscripts and letters, mine among others," that did not belong to him, but none of his victims in that instance appears to have preferred charges against him.

Miles Lunatic Asylum, also called Hoxton House, was a private madhouse kept by Sir Jonathan Miles at Hoxton, north of the City. According to one authority (Coombs, 45), "A certificate of madness was easily obtained, and anyone was admitted so long as they, or their families, kept up the fees. . . . Criminals sought refuge [there] from the police." Montagu Gosset, one of the doctors who certified that Powell was insane, was a well-known surgeon with offices in the City. The other was Dr. Thomas Southwood Smith, who, among his many scientific and philanthropic activities, was chief founder of the Sanitorium on whose board Charles Dickens and Thomas Chapman served. As Powell was pleased to note in his sketch of Southwood Smith in his Living Authors of England *(95), "his good offices are always at the disposal of his friends."*

In 1886 Powell twice referred to Miles Lunatic Asylum in discussing Mary Lamb, who, suffering from periodic seizures of insanity (in one of which she knifed her mother to death), had been intermittantly confined there ("Leaves from My Life," 138, 493), as once had been her brother Charles. But on neither occasion did Powell mention his own confinement there. The Borough Archivist of the Hackney Archives Department reports: "Concerning Hoxton House, as far as we know the records of this institution have not survived."

Criminal cases in Surrey could be heard either before the Court of Quarter Sessions or at the Assizes. The County Archivist of the Surrey Record Office, which holds the records of the Quarter Sessions, writes: "I have consulted the Process Book for Quarter Sessions (QS 3/5/17) for this period [December 1848-January 1849] but can find no mention of a Thomas Powell in the index. I have also consulted the Calendars of Prisoners (QS 3/4/1) which include assize prisoners but these are incomplete and once again I can find no references to Thomas Powell."

The Public Record Office reports: "This Office holds the records of the Surrey Assizes, although the assizes for London and surrounding areas, from 1833, was the Central Criminal Court. This Office also holds the records of the Central Criminal Court, therefore [it is suggested] you search the Surrey Assizes and Central Criminal Court records for 1849." However, when the Croydon Assizes (ASSI 35/289/7, ASSI 35/289/8) and the Calendar for Central Criminal Court indictments for 1849 (CRIM 5/3) were searched, no reference to Thomas Powell was found.

Extraordinary Case.—On Saturday Mr. Shaw, the inspector of the P. division of police, made a communication to the magistrates of the Croydon district, in reference to a case which has been under consideration by them for several weeks, and the circumstances connected with which are of a very singular character. It appears that more than a month back, an application was made to the magistrates for a warrant to apprehend Mr. Thomas Powell, a gentleman who had been residing at Burgh-house, near Croydon, upon the charge of obtaining money by means of false checks, and one was accordingly placed in the hands of Mr. Shaw. He was, however, unable to meet with the defendant, but after the warrant had been granted a short time, Mr. Powell sent notice that he would attend at the police station on a certain day and be ready to answer any charge that might be preferred against him. He accordingly attended, and after a preliminary inquiry, the matter was adjourned until the following Saturday, bail being taken for the appearance of the defendant at the next bench day.

When the period arrived for the second examination, Mr. Powell did not appear, but Mr. Watts, of Old Broad-street, his solicitor, attended on his behalf, and put in a certificate signed by Dr. Southwood Smith, testifying that the defendant was in a dangerous state of illness; in fact, that he was insane, and utterly unfit to appear and undergo an examination; and the magistrates upon this consented to allow the case to stand over for a fortnight.

During this interval it was ascertained that there were several other cases in which the person accused had obtained money by means of forged checks, and from the information obtained by the police there also appeared very good reason for believing that, although the defendant was no doubt very ill, and that his brain was to some extent affected, yet that this state had been produced by artificial means—by the excessive use of opium, and resorting to the expedient of igniting charcoal in his bedroom, the object being to produce a temporary state of delirium, in the expectation by that means to evade justice.

When the day appointed for the second examination arrived, the defendant again failed to surrender, but his solicitor appeared for him, and Mr. Howard, of Norfolk-street, was also present as the professional adviser of the gentlemen who had become sureties for the accused.

Upon this occasion, to the surprise of the bench, it was stated by Mr. Watts that the defendant was in a lunatic asylum, raving mad, and the certificate of the keeper of Miles's Lunatic Asylum, at Hoxton, was produced, which stated that Mr. Powell had been admitted to that establishment upon a certificate of lunacy, signed by Dr. S. Smith and Dr. Montagu Gosset.

Mr. Adams, the chairman of the bench, expressed the surprise of the magistrates at this course of proceeding, and at the same time their determination not to allow the ends of justice to be defeated. The defendant's solicitor assured the bench that he was no party to such a proceeding and said that, by whatever means the madness of the defendant was occasioned, there could be no doubt of his being in that state, and that he was consequently quite unfit to undergo an examination or to be called upon to give any answer to the charge.

Mr. Howard then made an application to the bench to discharge the recognizances of Dr. Ryan and Mr. Machell [Powell's father-in-law], the gentlemen who had become sureties for the defendant surrendering himself. He said they were quite willing to perform the condition they had imposed upon themselves, and, as they were prevented from doing so by the act of God, he submitted to the bench that they were, under such circumstances, entitled to be relieved from further responsibility.

Mr. Sutherland, one of the magistrates, in answer to the application, said that the bench were not at all satisfied that the condition of the defendant was occasioned by the act of God, but, on the contrary, from the information they had received, they had good reason to believe that the defendant, by the use of opium and other means, had reduced himself to his present condition, in the expectation that he would be enabled by this proceeding to evade justice. If such were the case, the illness would probably be only temporary, and under such circumstances they could not think of relieving the bail from the responsibility they had incurred of producing the defendant.

After some further discussion, the magistrates enlarged the recognizances of the bail, and the matter was ordered to stand over, directions being given to the police to make the necessary inquiries for the satisfaction of the bench. The inspector now reported that he had been to the asylum where the accused gentleman was confined, and had been admitted to see him, and he was evidently at present in a state of insanity; but he said he had received an assurance that the moment his condition improved, so as to enable him to undergo an examination, he should be brought before the bench; and he had also taken other measures to insure this result and prevent a failure of justice. Thus the matter stands at present, the case having, from the singular nature of the proceedings connected with it and the position in life of the defendant, created a good deal of interest.

---

20. *23 January 1849: Disclaimer from a Thomas Powell*

Editor of The Times

Thomas Powell is a very common name. According to the fragmentary data collected by the International Genealogical Index, there were thirty Thomas Powells born in the British Isles in the year that the subject of "Extraordinary Case" (Document 19) was born. One of these many Thomas Powells lived just east of Croydon, and having no desire to be confused with the alleged forger and certified lunatic whose latest exploits had been reported in The Times, *he requested John T. Delane, the paper's editor, to inform his readers that he was not* that *Powell. Delane was considerate enough to comply.*

We are requested by Mr. Powell, of Woodside, near Croydon, to state that he is not the person of the same name who was implicated in the "Extraordinary Case" published by us some weeks hence.

---

21. *February 1880: Dr. Thomas Southwood Smith Certifies Thomas Powell To Be Insane*

R. H. Horne

Among Horne's posthumous papers is a manuscript letter addressed to the editor of the Daily News *which recounts his experiences with Powell. In a portion of the manuscript, here introduced and quoted by Horne's biographer (Blainey, 114), Horne reports on Dr. Smith's alleged account of his experience with Powell—alleged because the report is derisive and uncharacteristic of the good doctor.*

The manuscript is now in the Mitchell Library, Public Library of New South Wales, Sydney, Australia. (Seized by gold fever in 1852, Horne had gone to Australia, where he stayed until 1869. There, in his fifties, he lived with an eighteen-year-old woman, who bore him two children, both of whom died young. To his credit, he signed papers that he was an adulterer and a deserter so that his wife could secure a divorce, which she did.)

Dr. Smith's own statement regarding Powell's insanity appears in Document 52.

Smith certified Powell insane. And no wonder, if Horne's version can be believed, for, according to Horne, Smith arrived to find Powell in a suicidal fit—faked with laudanum and pepper—foaming at the mouth, his clothes disordered and face swollen, "standing on his head in one corner of the drawing-room, singing snatches of obscene songs."

THE VENDETTA BEGINS

"It will take a long time to do, but vengeance is strong, and Dickens persevering."
—Charles Dickens to Thomas Powell

22. *6 September 1849: "Charles Dickens" from Thomas Powell's* The Living Authors of England

New York Evening Post

That Thomas Powell, Houdini-like, was able to effect an escape from Miles Lunatic Asylum and to elude the surveillance of the Croydon police is bound to raise suspicions, inasmuch as a Police Inspector had assured the court that the moment Powell's condition improved, he would be brought back before the Bench. Moreover, the Inspector had informed the magistrates that "he had . . . taken other measures to insure this result, and prevent a failure of justice" (Document 19). Add to this that Powell managed to board a ship bound to New York with his wife and four children, and suspicion is redoubled. That feat could only have been executed if accomplices and pay-offs were involved. Indeed, John Allan, the junior partner in Chapman & Co., disclosed as much in reporting that Powell "was sent out of the country by his friends, as the only hope of retrieving his character" (Document 52). No doubt, the blot on the family escutcheon had to be removed, which may also explain why Powell's name does not appear in the various records specified in the Headnote to Document 19. (Ships' passenger lists, chiefly from Liverpool to New York, were scanned for the period to discover precisely when the Powells emigrated, but without success, for the lists often proved illegible due to poor or faded handwriting, and it is conceivable that the Powells may have used false names.)

With all this, Powell managed to write a book of 316 pages on thirty-eight literary figures ranging from Wordsworth to Jerrold, and, if this were not enough, within months of arriving in New York, he succeeded in inducing the respectable firm of D. Appleton & Co. to publish it.

A strange aspect of these events is that even The Times *did not cover Powell's escape and decampment, though that paper had shown great interest in Powell's bizarre affairs in its report, "Extraordinary Case" (Document 19).*

Robert Browning in later years wrote to a friend: Powell "was forced to fly the country, thereby avoiding the punishment he richly deserved. . . . He at once, on arriving in America, wrote a description of his 'literary friends.' This I never saw, but was assured, at the time [probably by Horne], that it was a sort of revenge on every one of them for being of good repute" (Hood, 257).

As for Powell's being the author of Florentine Tales, *the work attributed to him here by the* Evening Post, *"the evidence, internal and circumstantial, suggests that Hunt is the most likely author" (Fogle, 83). A half-year after being dismissed from Chapman & Co. as a forger and thief, Powell with supreme chutzpah inscribed a copy of* Florentine Tales *(published, no doubt, with embezzled funds) as follows: "To Mrs. Chapman/& Thos. Chapman Esq. F.R.S.T.Sh./this volume is presented by/the wretched & unhappy Author./Jany 2nd. 1847" (ibid., 79).*

Appleton, being an enterprising publisher, bombarded New York newspapers with a long extract from the chapter on Dickens. The Evening Post, *recognizing a sensational item which cost it nothing, spread the extract over three columns of its front page.*

Those passages that appeared in Living Authors of England *but not in this excerpt are indicated by braces. Trivial typographical differences (cheques for checks, for instance) exist between the newspaper and book versions. Typos have been silently corrected.*

The Living Authors of England

This is the title of a new work, soon to appear from the press of the Messrs. Appleton, written by Thomas Powell, an English gentleman, who is popularly known as the author of "Florentine Tales." It will embrace sketches of many of the most prominent literary celebrities of England now living, drawn by one of their number. From some proof sheets, with which we have been kindly favored by the publisher, we are permitted to make the following extracts from Mr. Powell's sketch of Dickens, which will be found to contain many new and interesting facts relating to the *personal* history of this favorite writer.

Charles Dickens

This popular author was born in February, 1812, at Rochester; and passed his early years beneath the shadow of that fine old well-preserved ruin, the castle, wandering on the banks of the Medway, or listening (we strongly suspect, outside) to the chaunting of the cathedral service.

His father, who was a clerk in the Chatham dock-yard, retiring on a pension some years after, came to London, where his celebrated son finished the little education he ever received; he was then articled to a solicitor in Bedford Row, where he formed the acquaintance of a reporter engaged in the "Morning Chronicle." He soon grew disgusted with the drudgery of the desk's "dead wood," and exchanged it for the more exciting life of the public press. He, therefore, became one of the staff of the leading liberal journals, the paper already named.

Here his sagacity, quickness, and, above all, his skill in seizing on the prominent features of a subject, made him one of their most useful attachés, and he was generally despatched to attend the most important political meetings.

In the "Chronicle" appeared those clever sketches which first made the name of "Boz" known to the world; this *soubriquet* he had given to his youngest brother, Augustus, whom he called Moses, which, corrupted into Boses, finally became "Boz," and, as a remembrance of fondness for the child, he resolved to adopt it as his literary name. These sketches are too well known to need any distinct criticism; the surprising minuteness of their details, the ingenuity with which he selects peculiarities, and by humorous exaggeration carries them into the world of caricature, made him at once the favorite author of those who read only to be amused. It may be doubted whether these sketches will not be his chiefest passport to fame in future times; unable to construct a symmetrical plot, his larger works grow tedious; compelled, by the very nature of his plan to publish his chapters separately, he has confined the artistic unity of his novel to the ephemeral necessity of producing something very piquant for every number; the great effects are, therefore, frittered away in the progress of the work, and the crowning interest of the climax is divided among twenty numbers, published at stated intervals: this unfortuante dilution of an originally strong article is avoided in his first production, and the "sketches" will probably always remain as a record of the life of the lower classes of England.

D. APPLETON & CO.
HAVE NOW READY:

THE
LIVING AUTHORS OF ENGLAND.

By THOMAS POWELL.

One volume 12 mo. Price $1, cloth.

CONTENTS:

William Wordsworth, Leigh Hunt, Thomas Moore, Cornwell, Landor, Rogers, Tennyson, Macaulay, Browning, Burbidge, Clough, Smith, Patmore, Domett, Taylor, Browning, Dickens, Talfourd, Jones, Milnes, Forster, Horne, Moxon, Carlyle, Mackay, Heraud, Bennett, Reade, Gurney, Marston, Stephens, Bailey, Knowles, Bulwer, Boucicault, Lovell, Jameson, Douglas Jerrold.

Ad in *The Literary World*

His next work was a smart brochure, entitled "Sunday under three heads," to which he placed the assumed name of "Timothy Sparks." Here he lays bare, with an unsparing hand, the hollowness of that pharisaical sect which endeavored, by legislation, to enforce the gloom of a puritanic fast on the christian's cheerful Sabbath. This work, which is not generally known, had prefixed to it an ironical dedication to the Bishop of London, who had rendered himself busy in the matter. There are many admirable sketches in this little volume, full of point and bitter truth: such as the description of a "fashionable congregation of miserable sinners," where the levity, foppery and millinerism of the whole assembly of "prayerful persons" are depicted with much power and sarcasm. A picture in this sketch, of a father fetching home the Sunday dinner from the baker's, with all his little ones hailing him as he comes up the street, within sight of his own door, is one of those graphic touches of low life which places Mr. Dickens far above all competition in that inferior class of writing. We have a great objection to this eternal painting with *mud*, instead of *colors*; introduced into a story as a part of the whole, it is an agreeable change and gives greater effect to the pathetic and loftier portions, as the scenes where Dogberry and Verges figure in Shakespere's drama of "Much ado about Nothing"; but when this is the entire staple, the work becomes degraded to a far lower style of art, and is not the representation of life, but only of a particular phase of it; a Hamlet of grave-diggers, or a Henry the Fifth, full of Nyms and Bardolphs, would be an equivalent in the world of letters to most, if not all, of Mr. Dickens' works.

The writing of "Pickwick" was one of those accidents which now and then happens in a "literary life"; it is, however, an absurdity to believe that had not this special opportunity occurred, the author of "Oliver Twist" would have waited for *circumstance* to make him a popular writer; his genius would have created the circumstance had it not been offered to him without the trouble of waiting. It is, however, strictly true that Mr. Dickens was at first engaged merely to illustrate the design of Mr. Seymour, the artist, who had formed the idea of ridiculing, in a series of engravings, that class of pompous dullnesses which strut about society in the peacock feathers of a few facts learned by rote, and which they consider and call learning; we are sometimes inclined to agree with Lamb, who, when asked by a member of the Royal Society to define learning, boldly answered, and maintained for a considerable time, that it was the systematic arrangement of ignorance—a grammar which all solemn fools quoted. Seymour thought that a club of Cockneys, travelling about geologizing, botanizing, gormandizing, and employed on other equally scientific pursuits, would be the most popular vehicle for satirizing that class of "emphatic nothings" which delight in the appendage to their name of F.R.S., A.S.S. or any other mysterious signs which they think have the magic power of bestowing learning or distinction. The melancholy termination of the caricaturist's career, soon, however, gave to Mr. Dickens the paramount voice in this joint work.

The suicide of Mr. Seymour was rendered doubly distressing to him, by the fact of his having dined with the novelist the very day in which he perpetrated this terrible deed of despair.

He had left Mr. Dickens' house after a merry evening, when he had pointed out to Mr. Seymour two passages in the new number which he wished illustrated. Next morning Mr. Dickens was surprised at receiving a very early visit from one of his publishers, Mr. Chapman. His manner was so agitated that the author's first impression was that he had come to announce a suspension of payment. "Good heavens," cried Mr. Dickens, "what is the matter?" Mr. Chapman's reply horrified him—"Poor Seymour has destroyed himself!" They both started for the ill fated artist's house, where they found the melancholy report was too true: there lay the hapless son of genius dead, and the cause of the rash act was perfectly apparent to them, for looking round his studio they saw many lithographic stones with the designs scarcely commenced, but which the sanguine sketcher had represented to his publishers as being nearly completed.

Mr. Dickens' solution of the mystery is, that on his return home from dining with him, the contemplation of the heavy arrears of works he had to do, operating on a quick nervous temperament, somewhat excited by wine, produced a temporary delirium, under which influence he destroyed himself. Every reader of Pickwick knows that Mr. Browne was engaged to complete the illustrations, and he has done it with such spirit and felicity that we venture to assert very much of Mr. Dickens' popularity is owing to the tangible shape in which the artist places the author: in a certain sense his rapid and graphic pencil lends to airy nothing a local habitation and a name.

Mr. Dickens' next work was Nicholas Nickleby, and during this he edited "Bentley's Magazine." Here he had a disagreement with the proprietor and retired from its management. He, however, finished, according to his agreement, the tale of Oliver Twist, which first appeared in this periodical. The dispute originated in the remuneration he received as editor. Mr. Bentley complains that he nearly doubled in less than a year the annual sum he had engaged to pay Dickens, and upon his hesitating to comply with another increased demand, he threw up the contract altogether.

The novel of Oliver Twist is certainly the finest piece of construction Mr. Dickens has given to the world, and notwithstanding the revolting picture it presents of part of human nature, there is little doubt but that its total effect has been beneficial.

We have been told by English magistrates that they had no idea of the infamous system then flourishing, till Dickens attacked it, pen in hand:—and several have declared that the recollection of Oliver Twist has compelled them to give a more patient and indulgent hearing to the unfortunate orphan, who tossed upon the world, falls into the hands of evil men, and becomes their dupe and their victim. In this work he also exposed the ignorance, brutality, and conceit of some of the paid officials of London, who are little better than an inferior kind of Jeffreys, men who bow to the titled or wealthy criminal, and who exhaust their indignation and legal vengeance on the weak and the destitute offender. The character of Mr. Fang in this novel was well known to be intended for Mr. Laing, the notorious Bow-street magistrate; and so conscious was he of the resemblance that it was currently rumored at the time that he wrote to "Boz," inquiring if he intended to personify him in this picture.

Report adds, that Mr. Dickens' reply stated, that Mr. Laing must be the best judge how far he felt the cap fitted him. On a later occasion Mr. Dickens told us that he intended to hold up to the scorn and detestation of his fellow citizens the conduct of Alderman Sir Peter Laurie, who, in the arrogance and stupidity of undeserved power declared he would "put suicide down"—as though the terrors of the law would have any effect on the phrensied spirit, who fearing not his God, rushed unannounced into his presence. When the "Chimes" appeared, the alderman Cute, in the book so admirably done, every one acknowledged, by acclamation, the likeness to Laurie. The astonished saddler roared out in the indignation and vexation of the moment, "I wonder Mr. Dickens is so ungrateful to attack me: I have always been civil to him, and didn't I, at the last Lord Mayor's ball, lead Mrs. Dickens down to dinner?"—Unhappy Cute! did not the gormandizing noodle see that when the wife of a man of genius condescends to honor such a man by accepting a personal attention, it is she who confers the favor, and renders him the obliged party!

The passage in the Chimes, in which the indignant author ridicules and denounces the blasphemous folly of putting human madness down, is powerfully written, and a good specimen of Mr. Dickens' best style. No man can write simpler and stronger English than the celebrated Boz, and this renders us the more annoyed at those manifold vulgarities and slipshod errors of style, which unhappily have of late years so disfigured his productions.

While we are on this point we may as well allude to the character of Dombey, the hero of Mr. Dickens' last completed monthly novel; this is well known as intended to represent a shipowner and merchant "not a hundred miles" from Leadenhall-street, in whose office a relative of the novelist is clerk.

The "little wooden midshipman" of Solomon Gills with his sextant in his untiring hand, with his one foot advanced, and his coat tails flying back, may be seen any day two or three doors down Leadenhall-street, and immediately facing the office of the self-satisfied and arrogant merchant who sat for the portrait of Dombey. When the first number appeared the likeness was readily recognized by this wealthy merchant's relatives, and he was christened Dombey on the spot; he himself was not averse to the "high distinction of being the hero of a work by so popular a writer as Mr. Dickens": we ourselves have seen him blandly smile as the allusion has been made in his hearing; but as the work proceeded, and the heartless mercenary character of a London mechant was unfolded, his face grew tragically dismal at the slightest reference to what had formerly fed his pride! Alas! poor little human nature, how dreadful to thy ear is the truth when presented by another!—well did the Scotch exciseman show his far-sighted knowledge of the heart of man when he wrote

"O would some gentle power gie us
To see ourselves as others see us!"

But perhaps in both cases it would only wound self-love, and not kill the slumbering devil! We cannot help in this place remarking, that when Mr. Dickens commenced "Dombey" he stated to several that, in his new work, it was his intention to expose the arrogance and pride of every English merchant, with an eye to the correction of those notorious vices. It is evident to all that he either lacked the courage or the power to achieve so great and praiseworthy an object. It has resulted in the miserable failure of grossly libelling and caricaturing one person, and thus narrowing a great public object to a private end. Had the castigator of the Yorkshire schoolmasters, the paid magistrates, the imposter architects, the dandy milliners and the grinding usurers, possessed the nerve to teach the arrogant merchants of London that their clerks and dependents were worthy better treatment than they receive at the hands of their Egyptian taskmasters, Mr. Dickens might have secured a fame which is fast fading away under his new dispensation of writing; but this narrowing of an originally fine and broad-viewed mind will always happen when an author deserts the manly code of his early years, and transforms himself into the companion of fashionable dandies, literary lords and heartless millionaires.

It is unnecessary to follow, seriatim, the progress of so well known a writer. His works are familiar to all, and we shall, therefore, confine ourselves to a few critical remarks on his remaining productions.

Few writers of modern times equal Mr. Dickens in the fidelity with which he selects some family in low life, and paints their portraits; they are complete Dutch pictures; even the tone of voice, and the look are given, the Crummles, the Kenwigs, and the Squeers, are daguerreotyped for posterity with an unerring accuracy. When, however, he ventures upon the loftier and more complex phases of human nature, he miserably fails, and evidences at once that want of universality which renders him, perhaps, one of the most one-sided delineators of the human family that ever enjoyed a popular reputation. His want of success in this department was once illustrated by a sarcastic writer, as reminding him of the story of the scavenger.

An old master in that, the dirtiest of sciences, was asked one day his opinion of a new and popular apprentice he had.

Scratching his head, and looking very profound, he uttered in an oracular tone of voice, "In a straightfor'ard piece of business, such as sweeping a crossing, he was undeniably great, but when he came to a little dainty bit, a loftier kind of fancy work, such as tittivating round a post, he showed a sad *want of genius*"; so with Dickens in low characters; he is wonderfully true, graphic and amusing; but when he comes to a little dainty piece of portraiture, such as a gentleman, or a young lady of birth, breeding, or fashion, or indeed of any heroic character, he shows a deficiency of power both in conception and execution which materially diminishes his chance with posterity.

{His powers of description seem to stop short at Cockneys; his heroes are generally men-milliners, and his heroines lackadaisical and artificially virtuous nursery maids. He seems to be in an ever-lasting scuffle with schoolmaster and boarding-house keepers; and though these are perhaps two very disgusting specimens, we do not think they ought to form the Alpha and Omega of mankind; a writer whose staple is of this quality will soon exhaust the patience of the critics and lower the standard of his readers.

We notice, with much regret, that a tyrannical schoolmaster is a prominent character in his present work, "Copperfield"; surely we have had more than enough of Squeers, Blimbers, and Creakles. Mr. Dickens herein becomes the libeller. A survey of his works would lead to the infallible conclusion that all the instructors of youth were bad; we believe that so far as Mr. Dickens' own experience of the schoolmaster is concerned it is very limited; we do not mean this reproachfully to our distinguished countryman; a moment's reflection must convince every one that in proportion as art has done little for him, nature has done more; but we merely quote it as a singular instance of Mr. Dickens' being unable to get beyond his own experience; he can only describe; what he has seen he can tell; the retina of his wonderfully observant eye is perfect; his organ of language is full; the scene is brought before you, heightened into piquancy by his powers of exaggeration; but here he stops. He has no imagination; he is, in a word, a daguerreotypist, not a great painter.

If this estimate be correct, it necessarily places the author of Pickwick in the second class of literature, and even here not as the first, so long as Fielding remains to contest the point. That he exceeds Smollett we feel assured, from a certain instinct more unerring than all the logical deduction in the world; but so long as breadth and boldness of sketching, force of expression, naturalness and brilliancy of coloring are regarded, the author of Tom Jones will always be considered the chief in this department of literature. With reference to the unfairness of Mr. Dickens to schoolmasters, we must be allowed to offer our own experience against his. Our school recollections are the pleasantest part of our existence, and we hear few names pronounced with more pleasure and gratitude than those of Thelwall, Alvey, Gaunt, and Rachham, the names of our schoolboy masters.

It is impossible to avoid noticing the strong family likeness existing between the writings of an American author and Mr. Dickens. When this was first pointed out to us, with true English partiality we, of course, unhesitatingly pronounced him to be an imitator of the author of Pickwick. We were, therefore, proportionably surprised when, on comparing dates, we found that the American, although a much younger man, was in the field before his brother Englishman. It would not be just to accuse Mr. Dickens of being an imitator of the transatlantic writer; but the coincidence is curious, and as such we invite the attention of our readers to the parallel passages. The style is somewhat different, to be sure; but with all our English prepossessions we are forced to give the preference to the American; for it will be seen that the latter completes his picture in fewer strokes, is quite as graphic, without being so ultra a caricaturist, and has a bolder and more philosophical mind.

Alas! that I should write it! but our friends on the other side the water applaud the author of Pickwick to the echo, but leave their own countryman in comparative obscurity. America will always want the highest element of a great and enduring nation, so long as she condescends to steal the literature of England, rather than pay her own undoubted men of genius. With regard to these extracts, we have only to observe, that the humor of the American writer is infinitely more universal than that of the English one. There is nothing comic in the abstraction of a poor child's dinner by a waiter, who had the physical force to take it if he felt so inclined, while we can conceive nothing more Shakesperian in its humor than the picture presented of a full grown evening party standing by while a gormandizing functionary devours before their eyes the great bulk of the delicacies provided for their evening's entertainment. The humor in the latter case is heightened by the consciousness that they have indirectly brought it on themselves by their obsequious deference to the voracious alderman. The picture is admirably drawn, and notwithstanding the laughter it must ever occasion to the reader, we defy any critic to put his pen upon a single line, and say it is exaggerated.

We offer them both to the critical judgment of any impartial critic, be he American or English.

> "'There's half a pint of ale for you. Will you have it now?'
>
> "I thanked him, and said 'Yes.' Upon which he poured it out of a jug into a large tumbler, and held it up against the light, and made it look beautiful.
>
> "'My eye!' he said. 'It seems a good deal, don't it?'
>
> "'It does seem a good deal,' I answered, with a smile. For it was quite delightful to me to find him so pleasant. He was a twinkling-eyed, pimple-faced man, with his hair standing upright all over his head; and as he stood with one arm a-kimbo, holding up the glass to the light with the other hand, he looked quite friendly.
>
> "'There was a gentleman here, yesterday,' he said, 'a stout gentleman, by the name of Topsawyer—perhaps you know him!'
>
> "'No,' I said, 'I don't think—'
>
> "'In breeches and gaiters, broad-brimmed hat, grey coat, speckled choaker,' said the waiter.
>
> "'No,' I said bashfully, 'I haven't the pleasure—'
>
> "'He came in here,' said the waiter, looking at the light through the tumbler, 'ordered a glass of this ale—*would* order it—I told him not—drank it, and fell dead. It was too old for him. It oughtn't to be drawn; that's the fact.'
>
> "I was very much shocked to hear of this melancholy accident, and said I thought I had better have some water.
>
> "'Why you see,' said the waiter, still looking at the light through the tumbler, with one of his eyes shut up, 'our people don't like things being ordered and left. It offends 'em. But I'll drink it, if you like. I'm used to it, and use is everything. I don't think it'll hurt me, if I throw my head back, and take it off quick. Shall I?'
>
> "I replied that he would much oblige me by drinking it, if he thought he could do it safely, but by no means otherwise. When he did throw his head back, and take if off quick, I had a horrible fear, I confess, of seeing him meet the fate of the lamented Mr. Topsawyer, and fall lifeless on the carpet. But it didn't

hurt him. On the contrary, I thought he seemed the fresher for it.

"'What have we got here?' he said, putting a fork into my dish. 'Not chops?'

"'Chops,' I said.

"'Lord bless my soul!' he exclaimed, 'I didn't know they were chops. Why, a chop's the very thing to take off the bad effects of that beer! Ain't it lucky?'

"So he took a chop by the bone in one hand, and a potato in the other, and ate away with a very good appetite, to my extreme satisfaction. He afterwards took another chop, and another potato; and after that, another chop and another potato. When we had done, he brought me a pudding, and having set it before me, seemed to ruminate, and to become absent in his mind for some moments.

"'How's the pie?' he said, rousing himself.

"'It's a pudding,' I made answer.

"'Pudding?' he exclaimed. 'Why, bless me, so it is! What!' looking at it nearer. 'You don't mean to say it's a batter pudding!'

"'Yes, it is indeed.'

"'Why, a batter pudding,' he said, taking up a table-spoon, 'is my favorite pudding! Ain't that lucky? Come on, little 'un, and let's see who'll get most.'

"The waiter certainly got most. He entreated me more than once to come in and win, but what with his table-spoon to my tea-spoon, his dispatch to my dispatch, and his appetite to my appetite, I was left far behind at the first mouthful, and had no chance with him. I never saw any one enjoy a pudding so much, I think; and he laughed, when it was all gone, as if his enjoyment of it lasted still."

Copperfield, Chap. V.

"The walls of the parlor upon which he had entered were lined all round with well-dressed ladies and gentlemen, sitting as erect as corpses, and gazing into the empty space in the middle of the apartment, as if some curious meteorological phenomenon were going on there, in which they all had a special interest. At the announcement of Puffer Hopkins by a pale young gentleman at the door, the corpses waked up a little, some twittered spasmodically, a few moved uneasily in their chairs, and by the time Puffer had attained a seat in the corner, the company had again subsided into its condition of tomb-like repose.

"They were presently, however, again wakened, and with rather more success, by the entrance of the host, Mr. Fishblatt himself, bearing before him, firstly, a huge ruffle, which stood straight out from his bosom like a mainsail, and secondly, reposing in the shadow of the said ruffle, a black teaboard of proportionate dimensions, garnished with small jugs or tumblers of lemonade.

"Mr. Fishblatt walked very erect and majestically, and holding the waiter at arms' length, smiling pleasantly, as a gentleman always does when he's engaged in a business he knows himself to be altogether too good for, but which the crisis of affairs requires him to look after, presented it to the ladies all around, beginning at the left hand, as he was bound to do, and skipping ever so many thirsty gentlemen who gloated on the small jugs; and then coming down toward the right hand, as he was likewise bound, he allowed the thirsty gentlemen to glean from the waiter the tumblers that remained. It is not to be supposed that Mr. Halsey Fishblatt all this time held his peace; on the contrary, the bearing of the waiter was not a tithe of his toils, for he kept strenuously urging, wherever he went, the propriety of taking a tumbler, the necessity of a draught of the lemonade to cool themselves, and particularly soliciting and entreating the ladies to make a paradise of his (Mr. Fishblatt's) parlors, by enjoying themselves with all their might and main.

"The lemonade had scarcely vanished, and the empty tumblers been gathered and borne out of sight, when it was announced, to the discomfiture and confusion of the company, that the celebrated and distinguished representative of the thirteenth ward in the city councils, Alderman Punchwind, by name, was in the house, having, as it was understood, done Mr. Fishblatt the honor to call in and partake of the agreeable hospitalities that were then and there going forward. Mr. Fishblatt, at the thought of so august a presence, recoiled a little, but recovering speedily, a deputation was immediately sent out, consisting of Puffer Hopkins and two young gentlemen who wore large watch seals and were rather ambitious of office and employment of this kind, to wait upon his eminence. In a few minutes a heavy tread was heard upon the stair, a commotion in the entry, and in stalked, in a broad-brimmed hat, a portly, capacious, and solid gentleman, of such dimensions as to resemble not a little a great school-globe, stepped out of its brass ring, and taking a walk of pleasure.

"In he marched, accompanied by his delegation, who clung close to his skirts to watch the impression his presence might make on the commonalty assembled.

"Puffer Hopkins had a glimmering reminiscence of a broad-brimmed hat, very much like the alderman's escaping into a pantry at the end of the hall as he came in at the beginning of the evening, worn by Crump—could it be so? Crump, the meek secretary who had been so browbeaten in the shower by Mr. Blinker. His brows overshadowed by the huge hat, and his chin buried in a capacious collar, Alderman Punchwind paused for a minute at the door, glanced about slowly and with an air of solemn importance, and then, without removing his hat or uttering a word, stalked across the parlor, proceeded to fill a glass from the sideboard, where relays of refreshments in liberal quantities were arranged, and at this moment, deigning to turn around and recognise the company, he intimated by a look that he would drink all their good healths; which he did, very emphatically, absorbing his wine much as the Norwegian Maelstrom might, if it were a corporate alderman and fed at the public charge. Having disposed of the wine the alderman next devoted his attention to the cake and other eatables, of which great batches disappeared from time to time; with a pause now and then, to allow him to vary the entertainment with a friendly return, just to show he hadn't forgotten it, to the decanter; which proceedings were watched with painful interest by Mr. Fishblatt's guests—who were horrified at the miraculous disappearance of the provisions for the party and who looked upon the performance much as they would at the elephant at the managerie, feeding with a bale or two of hay, or the pagan anaconda at the museum, lunching on a pair of fowls and a live rabbit, without so much as a grace to the meal.

"As soon as Alderman Punchwind had concluded his corporate banquet by stripping the board of something more than two-thirds of its contents, solid and liquid, he wiped his lips, and marching steadily toward the centre of the rooms, there planted himself by the side of a column and looked abroad upon the company, fixing his eye, now and then, with peculiar sternness, on some young lady who happened to be fairer than her neighbors.

"After he had enjoyed this recreation for some time, various members of the company were brought up by Mr. Fishblatt, and introduced (by consent) to the distinguished functionary, who kept his ground manfully and received them all with an air of bland and gracious

> condescension; allowing each of them to take him by the hand, and to enjoy a few minutes' contemplation of his very classic and expressive features, and then pass off, making room for others."
>
> *Puffer Hopkins, Chap. IX.*

We do not mean, nor wish to detract from the well deserved reputation of Mr. Dickens—all we ask is fair play for every author, there is room enough in the world for all! We shall conclude this by observing, in order to prevent the possibility of any retort, that the American alderman's gobbling up the destined feast of the evening party, had five years the start of the waiter's feat in Copperfield. We shall treat more of these accidental coincidences when we come to consider the writings of Cornelius Mathews in their proper place.

To return to Mr. Dickens:—it would be a curious study to go carefully through the works of every popular author, and trace the predominance of that peculiarity or excellence which first brought him into notice: having contrasted Mr. Dickens with an American contemporary, and found that there could be no imitation in the matter, more especially on the other side of the Atlantic, we will compare him with an English author with whom he is on familiar terms.

A leading distinction between Dickens and Thackeray is the *coolness* of the latter compared with the partisanship of the other. Thackeray is a calm, observant, indifferent spectator, with a man of the world's aspect for the conventionals of life, and in spite of his sarcasms it is evident he entertains the opinion of Candide, that this is the best of all possible worlds. His paradise is a club life, with ragouts, parties and the most *recherche* of wines! His bower of bliss is an opera box. He looks at mankind through a lorgnette as he lounges on his seat, or enjoys the distinction of being safely ensconced in the Athenaeum, while he observes the mob pass by the window.

Dickens is a poet and a zealot—with more humor than wit, and is totally destitute of sarcasm. He can vituperate, not sneer! and like most humorists, he has a tendency to exaggeration. We all know that a certain degree of exaggeration is necessary to get the reader up to the author's mark, but we maintain that Mr. Dickens magnifies till it becomes so apparent as to expose itself. It may be necessary for an actress to rouge to a certain extent to counteract the ghastly effect of the broad stage-lights on the human countenance, but what should we say of her who daubed it on indiscriminately and unsparingly, giving as much to the nose as the check? So with the author, he composes in a glow, and beholds things immensely brighter than it will appear to the coldness, stupidity, or apathy of the common reader! Mr. Dickens' humor is Falstaffian, we admit, but he too frequently stuffs the fine old knight so much as to make him little better than a heap of old clothes; he buries the man in the buck basket truly, but he also requires him to wear them content, but like the grave-digger in Hamlet, he has too many waistcoats to be funny. Still there is heart and feeling in all this, and while the judicious blame the artist for his sacrifice of truth and nature, they laugh at the outrageousness of the distortion. Thackeray, on the other hand, never loses his temper or his judgment; Dickens often does: both scourge the offender, but the first does it from liking the office, and the other because he is angry, and thinks the culprit deserves it. In Vanity Fair the lash is always ringing on the back of the unhappy victim, but it is applied with the calculating prudence of the slave-driver, with a physician's regard for the life of the subject: he keeps him alive for further operations, and for future punishment. Dickens batters his opponent in a passion and gives up when tired: he rails and vituperates all the time, while Thackeray, with more severity, tortures at leisure. Both fish: but one pulls his trout out of the water at once and despatches it, while the other keeps it on the hook and drowns it by swimming. Dickens administers capital punishment on the spur of the moment; Thackeray imprisons for life, and racks his prisoner occasionally by way of amusement.

'Becky is as cold and wicked—as Quilp is a monstrous abortion—Thackeray is a Mephistopheles; Dickens a Faust!—One has most head, the other most heart! Both are great observers, but they look different ways. The observation of Thackeray is particular, that of Dickens general; while one is content to regard only the artificial, the other narrowly chronicles the natural.

A modern critic [Horne] has called Mr. Dickens the Hogarth of authors, and we think the epithet one of which the novelist may well be proud. In "Oliver Twist" we are perpetually reminded of the fact, and we can conceive nothing more perfect in the way of amusement than a novel written by Charles Dickens in his best manner, and illustrated by William Hogarth!

Among the scenes of that great fiction, one of the most touching things we ever read, is the scene where the poor sweet-hearted consumptive child, who is weeding the garden before any one else has risen, climbs up the gate, and putting his little arms through, clasps Oliver round the neck wishing him "good bye" with a brother's kiss. They had both been beaten and starved together, and in the little child's "good bye—God bless you," rushed a world of thought, and old feelings enough to drown the voice of a poor law commissioner in tears.

It is in touches like this that Mr. Dickens is so superior to the rest of his contemporaries: he often conveys a crowd of associations in a line, but too often takes a page to reiterate what destroys the whole effect of his previous effort. He leaves nothing to the reader's imagination: indeed he so overpaints his picture as not unfrequently to obliterate the original and successful design. Numberless instances of this might be given: we content ourselves by calling the reader's attention to the description of Ruth's pudding making, too well known to quote.}

[Here Powell interpolates an extended anecdote concerning William Charles Macready, the famous English tragedian, an anecdote totally irrelevant to his discussion of Dickens.]

In 1836 Mr. Dickens married Miss Catherine Hogarth, and to all human appearance the union has been a happy one; they have a family of seven children, the eldest a boy of about twelve years. His two last boys he has named after Alfred Tennyson and Francis Jeffreys, a piece of vanity unworthy so shrewd an observer of human nature.

In 1843 [1842] he visited America, but this is too well known to need any reference beyond the mere fact. We may, however, say in passing, that much of the unsatisfactory nature of that visit is chargeable to the injudicious course taken by the very respectable body of gentlemen, who, totally ignorant of the peculiar temperament of the distinguished novelist, somewhat officiously, though doubtless with the best intentions, took charge of him, and, in short, placed him under a complete *surveillance*, which impeded that free observation and genial intercourse with the masses which is absolutely necessary to the formation of a just opinion of the American people.

He has since passed a year in Italy, and another in Switzerland. He is fond of a trip to Paris, but the volatile manners of that vivacious nation seem to escape him, or baffle his powers of fixing on the canvas. It may be that he is unable to depict the finer traits of more polished life, and therefore wisely chooses the coarser and more boldly developed features of English and

American manners to paint from; be it as it may, it is only as a sketcher of low life that he will descend to future times, and in this point of view he will be valuable to the future dramatist and historian to supply them with the manners and peculiarities of that class of mankind which constitute the majority of the human race.

Mr. Dickens in private life is good-tempered and hospitable; he has a striking face; his hair is dark and long; his eye, which is the great fact of his countenance, is hazel; he is rather under the middle size, is neatly made, and very active; his favorite time for composition is in the morning; he writes till about one or two; lunches, than takes a walk for a couple of hours, returns to dinner, and gives the evening to his own or a friend's fireside.

He is a very gay dresser—eschews collars—rejoices in bright scarlet rolling facings to his waistcoat—is as fond of rings and gold chains as a Mosaic Jew. Indeed he dresses in a manner which, if indulged in by another, would inevitably call forth some of his genial banter. He is fond of country dances and similar amusements. By his own fireside he is as pleasant and companionable as his warmest admirer could wish: his conversation, however, is not what might be expected from a man so justly celebrated: he tells a story well, and with ever fresh variations or humorous exaggerations. He is a strong admirer of Tennyson and Browning; we have heard him declare that he would rather have written the "Blot in the 'Scutcheon" than any work of modern times. We have heard similar high admiration expressed on the other side of the Atlantic. Taking this for what it is worth, it still shows how highly that unpopular poet is esteemed by some of the leading intellects of England and America.

Mr. Dickens lives in good style in the Regent's Park, and is reported to live "not too wisely, but too well." Men of quick feelings and ardent sympathies are not expected to be Cocker's Arithmetic in the flesh, or to have the calculating mind of a London or a New-York merchant.

He abominates argument; delights in walking the crowded thoroughfares of life, and noting the humors of his fellow-creatures. He has a strong sympathy with all the oppressed classes, and has no toleration for the misanthrope or the cold-hearted aristocrat. He now and then administers a little gentle rebuke to affectation, in a pleasant but unmistakeable manner.

We remember an instance where he silenced a bilious young writer, who was inveighing against the world in a very "forcible, feeble manner"; during a pause in this philippic against the human race, Dickens said across the table, in the most self-congratulatory of tones: "I say, _____, what a lucky thing it is you and I don't belong to it? It reminds me," continued the author of Pickwick, "of the two men, who on a *raised* scaffold were awaiting the final delicate attention of the hangman; the notice of one was aroused by observing that a bull had got into the crowd of spectators, and was busily employed in tossing one here, and another there; whereupon one of the criminals said to the other, 'I say, Bill, how *lucky it is* for us that we *are up here*.'"

In general, however, his remarks are not happy. Notwithstanding this apparent theoretical sympathy with the lower classes, he pays an absurd deference to men of rank, and thinks no dinner table complete without a lord, or a very rich merchant or banker. This has been decidedly injurious to his writings; it has cramped his hand "and checked the thunder in mid volley."

A little anecdote will illustrate this "amiable weakness" better than a lengthened disquisition.

An acquaintance of his, calling one morning upon a celebrated writer, distinguished for his plain speaking, was astonished by the latter saying, in his most plaintive Scotch, in the course of conversation, "Poor Dickens! I am sorry for him; I could have better spared a better mon!" "You amaze me," replied the other, "why, I saw him last week, in good health. For God's sake tell me all about it—when did he die?" "Die, mon!" roared the philosopher, "I never said he was dead; I meant that it was all over with him as a great author." "What do you mean?" inquired the visitor. "Why, I mean this, he has dined with a real live lord, and it's in the newspapers! I say again, I am truly sorry for poor Dickens!"

His most intimate companions are Mr. Macready, Forster, Rogers, Landon, Harley and Talfourd; his acquaintance, however, extends throughout the whole range of the literary circles.

Notwithstanding the attention he receives from a few of the nobility, such as Earl Carlisle, Denman and Ashley, he is unpopular with the fashionable circles, and is merely asked as they would invite Tom Thumb, the Siamese Twins, or any other lusus naturae, merely to increase the dramatic attractions of the evening; but the weakness of feeling flattered by the attentions of rank or wealth, is a common failing with most men, especially when they have sprung from a humble class in society, and where the mind is deficient in the highest qualities, or not fortified by great self-respect; of this latter requisite, Mr. Dickens has less than most men so widely renowned.

To sum up his capabilities in a few words: as a man, he is good-tempered, vain, fickle, which makes him at times appear to be insincere; on the other hand, it must in justice be stated that he forgets with kindly facility an offence; but the impression on the minds of those who have known him longest is, that he is deficient in all those striking qualities of the heart which sanctify the memory of man. As an author, we have given our opinion of him, and stated our reasons. A few years will probably modify his position as compared with such writers as Carlyle, Browning, Tennyson, Miss Barrett, Bailey, and many other of his contemporaries. He will, however, always hold a commanding position in his own peculiar department of composition.

We must not forget to mention that, misled by his fame, Mr. Dickens tried his hand on dramatic composition, and wrote a farce, which was acted at the Lyceum. As might be expected, from his want of constructive power it was unequivocally condemned; this settles the question as to the author of Copperfield being a writer of the first class. It is a curious fact that all the first intellects of the age have been progressive; now with the writer before us, his first two works are unmistakeably his best.

In 1846 Mr. Dickens was persuaded by some friends to become the editor of a newspaper called the "Daily News," then about to be established as a rival to the "Times," on the liberal side of politics. On January 26th, of that year, the first number appeared, but after conducting it for three or four weeks the novelist found the pursuit distasteful, and retired from its management. It was said, at the time, that his salary was one hundred [actually thirty-eight] pounds per week, an amount equal, we are told, to an *entire year's* pay of many men of talent for editing leading daily papers in New-York.

---

23. *10 & 11 September 1849: Two Passages on "Police Intelligence"—Thomas Powell Charged with Fraud*

New York Herald

Just as newspapers were publishing extracts on Dickens from Powell's forthcoming book on Living Authors of England, *Powell was arrested for fraud. Two such items appeared in the* Herald.

John Allan was the junior partner of Chapman & Co.

Officer Calrow, one of the chief's aides, arrested last evening a respectable looking man by the name of Thomas Powell residing at the corner of Soho street and Broadway, of a warrant issued by Justice McGrath wherein Mr. Powell is charged with drawing a bill of exchange for £100 sterling on John Allan of London, dated the 15th of July last, which bill has been returned protested for nonpayment. Mr. Powell, it seems, obtained an advance of some $200 on this draft from Messrs. Richard Bell and McLaughlan brokers, corner of Hanover and Exchange place; and now, on the return of the bill protested, and from other advices sent from London in reference to the same, Mr. Bell alleges that the accused at the time the money was advanced on the bill, was well aware that he was drawing on a house [Chapman & Co.] who would not honor his draft; whereby they have been defrauded out of the money so loaned or advanced on the bill of exchange. The case is to be further heard before the magistrate; in the meantime Mr. Powell is detained in custody.

We noticed, in yesterday's *Herald*, the arrest of Thomas Powell, on an alleged charge of passing a bill of exchange for £100 on the banking firm of Bell & McLaughlan which bill was returned protested. The case was heard yesterday morning before Justice McGrath, who dismissed the complaint, as the evidence produced did not substantiate the charge against the accused. Mr. Powell, therefore, was liberated from custody.

---

24. *15 September 1849: An Extract from Thomas Powell's* Living Authors of England *in the* Literary World

Evert A. Duyckinck

Duyckinck had served as editor for Wiley & Putnam's Library of Choice Reading (a series that reprinted British books) and their Library of American Books. Among those Americans he chose to publish were his friends Poe, Hawthorne, Melville, Simms, Caroline Kirkland, and Cornelius Mathews, the last of whom would soon become embroiled in the Dickens-Powell vendetta.

The thirty-five letters, all undated, from Thomas Powell to Evert Duyckinck (in the Duyckinck Collection of the New York Public Library) reveal that Powell had established a friendship with Duyckinck to the extent of continually borrowing piddling amounts of money from him, as well as books from his vast library, including David Copperfield *and John Forster's* Life of Goldsmith.

The New York Literary World, *which Duyckinck was now editing with his brother George, was devoted to literary reviews, though it spiced its pages with other matter, including literary gossip. It was considered the best literary weekly in the country. Now, like the New York* Evening Post, *it was happy to print the extract on Dickens from* Living Authors of England *(Document 22), though in shortened form and with a brief acknowledgment.*

Mr. Powell's "Living Authors of England," to be published immediately by the Appletons, furnishes us with the following—a portion of the author's sketch of Dickens, with an anecdote from the paper on Talfourd.

[The extract follows.]

---

25. *27 October 1849: Review of Thomas Powell's* Living Authors of England *in the* Literary World

Evert A. Duyckinck

Reviews like Duyckinck's were bound to intrigue readers and, indeed, it appears that Living Authors of England *was a popular seller, as Powell followed it in January 1850 with* Living Authors of America: First Series.

If Powell really believed, as he averred in his essay on Dickens (Document 22), that Dickens "forgets with kindly facility an offence"—the "offence" in this instance referring to Powell's attack on him in his book—he had not entirely feigned his seizure of lunacy. For as Dickens warned Powell six years earlier in a similar context: "It will take a long time to do, but attack on vengeance is strong, and Dickens persevering" (P, 3:579).

The *Living Authors of England* is one of those books which are sure to be talked about and find their way speedily into everybody's hands. Mr. Powell, who has evidently had admittance in the best literary circles of London, has very kindly, or shrewdly perhaps, undertaken the somewhat unwelcome task of informing our public more particularly than had been done before respecting the characteristics and personal peculiarities of some of the lions and lesser beasts in that great menagerie. Having been so often in their cages, seen them at feeding-time, heard them roar, and listened to their growlings one with another, he has now assumed the office of showman. If many of the great *feles* and *canes* [felines and canines] were as sensitive as their namesakes of the forest, it would be well that he were cautioned how he again lets himself be seen in their vicinity, after having made so free with them; but your London lion is not a very "fearful wild fowl"; he is used to being feasted and caressed and petted, and to hear himself talked about—of all animals he is probably the least regardful of what is remarked upon him. Hence it is possible that Mr. Dickens, for example, will not be nettled at knowing it to be commonly reported that he lives "not wisely but too well"; and will still feel disposed to recognise as only a pleasant acquaintance who . . . thus "sums up his capabilities in a few words":—

"As a man, he is good-tempered, vain, fickle, which makes him at times appear to be insincere; on the other hand it must in justice be stated, that he forgets with kindly facility an offence; but the impression on the minds of those who have known him longest is, that he is deficient in all those striking qualities of the heart which sanctify the memory of man."

We are certainly indebted to Mr. Powell for a very alluring gossipy volume, upon matters and persons concerning which we cannot avoid feeling the greatest curiosity; it is written carefully, but is always lively, inviting, and in a sort, suggestive. We can already anticipate the encomiums of the press; we foreknow that these sketches will be unanimously pronounced "racy," if not "brilliant"; "readable" will not be strong enough. . . .

[Here Duyckinck quotes passages from Powell's introductory chapter to illustrate the author's "general discursive manner," then provides examples of the "anecdote and tattle" involving, among others, Hunt, Tennyson, Browning, and Carlyle, that, he predicts, will make Powell's work popular.]

But we have sufficiently multiplied our quotations from a volume which will soon be widely known. Mr. Powell promises us a similar one on American writers; we hope he will not forget our kind caution above written, and that while he writes just as freely as if he were a born Jonathan, he may be careful not to overstep or even approach the limit of polite usage. There are many passages in the present work which he will by and by regret having written—many which are open to more severe criticism than is our province or wish to apply, which are at variance with conventional courtesy; we are sure he will never regret the endeavor to avoid such in any work he may produce hereafter.

---

26. *October 1849: A Reference to* Living Authors of England *in the "Editor's Table" of the* Knickerbocker Magazine

Lewis Gaylord Clark

The "Editor's Table," which comprised "Gossip with our readers and correspondents," was a very popular section of the Knickerbocker, *a monthly magazine owned and edited by Clark. Clark greatly admired Dickens, whom he had met and entertained in 1842 when Boz was in the States gathering material for his* American Notes. *Clark was always hopeful that Dickens would honor his magazine with a contribution or two, but Dickens had his own magazines—first* Household Words, *then* All the Year Round*—to look out for.*

Oddly enough, Clark refers to Living Authors of England *as* British Writers, *and though he promises to review the book in November, the notice never appeared, for he was soon to hear from Dickens on that score (Document 28).*

We have received, and shall take occasion to notice in our next number, a volume entitled '*British Writers*,' by Mr. Thomas Powell. A hasty glance over its pages assures us of much material, deftly employed.

---

27. *20 October 1849: From a Letter to Thomas Chapman*

Charles Dickens

The excerpt from Living Authors of England *that Dickens refers to as "new proof of the villainy and unblushing falsehood of that execrable rascal Powell" appears as Document 22. As his statement makes evident, Dickens was no longer compassionate about Powell or prepared to cite the New Testament on temptation in pity of him (Document 10), now that he was Powell's latest victim.*

There was a great deal in the excerpt to gravel Dickens, but the passage that seemed to irk him most was the one in which Powell identified Mr. Dombey with Mr. Chapman—viz.: "We . . . allude to the character of Dombey," wrote Powell, "the hero of Mr. Dickens' last completed monthly novel; this is well known as intended to represent a shipowner and merchant . . . in whose office a relative of the novelist [Augustus] is clerk.

"The 'little wooden midshipman' of Solomon Gills with his sextant in his untiring hand, with his one foot advanced, and his coat tails flying back, may be seen any day two or three doors down Leadenhall-street, and immediately facing the office of the self-satisfied and arrogant merchant who sat for the portrait of Dombey. When the first number appeared the likeness was readily recognized by this wealthy merchant's relatives, and he was christened Dombey on the spot; he himself was not averse to the 'high distinction of being the hero of a work by so popular a writer as Mr. Dickens': we ourselves have seen him blandly smile as the allusion has been made in his hearing; but as the work proceeded, and the heartless mercenary character of a London merchant was unfolded, his face grew tragically dismal at the slightest reference to what had formerly fed his pride! . . . .

"We cannot help in this place remarking, that when Mr. Dickens commenced 'Dombey' he stated to several that . . . it was his intention to expose the arrogance and pride of every English

merchant, with an eye to the correction of those notorious vices. It is evident to all that he either lacked the courage or the power to achieve so great and praiseworthy an object. It has resulted in the miserable failure of grossly libelling and caricaturing one person, and thus narrowing a great public object to a private end. Had the castigator of the Yorkshire schoolmasters, the paid magistrates, the imposter architects, the dandy milliners and the grinding usurers, possessed the nerve to teach the arrogant merchants of London that their clerks and dependents were worthy better treatment than they receive at the hands of their Egyptian taskmasters, Mr. Dickens might have secured a fame which is fast fading away under his new dispensation of writing; but this narrowing of an originally fine and broad-viewed mind will always happen when an author deserts the manly code of his early years, and transforms himself into the companion of fashionable dandies, literary lords and heartless millionaires."

What was probably not lost on Powell, as apparently it has been on everyone else since, is that Dickens had reinforced the impression of the Dombey-Chapman relationship by situating Dombey's house "in the region between Portland-place and Bryanstone-square" (Ch. 3), though he knew that Chapman lived only a mile away at 14 Montagu-place, Bryanston-square. (Dickens sometimes addressed letters to Chapman with a final -e on Bryanston and Montagu.) For those interested in such details, the manuscript of Dombey and Son *shows that Dickens first chose Cavendish, then Portland Mall, before settling for Portland-place in the proofs.) If this telltale sign was not identifying enough, Dickens also made Dombey's residence, like Chapman's, "a corner-house" (Chs. 18 & 51). In the section titled "Street Directory" of Kelly's* Post Office London Directory, 1847, *No. 14 is listed as the last house on Montagu-place, just off Bryanston-square.*

It would have been natural for Dickens to model the firm of Dombey & Son upon Chapman & Co., inasmuch as his brother Augustus and his then friend Powell worked there in the counting-house, and he no doubt dropped in on them from time to time, as was common enough in those days. So casual were such visits that Powell recollected in a memoir, written when he was dying of Bright's disease, that "Mr. Wordsworth called on me at my uncle's place of business in Leadenhall Street, and asked me to pilot him to Clement's Lane, where he had an appointment to meet his old friend [Samuel] Rogers"

("Leaves from My Life," 135). There is also the story that Dickens often dropped in on Thomas Chapman when Lloyd's Registry had offices at No. 2, White Lion Court (Blake, 171).

If there was much to gravel Dickens in Powell's essay on him, there was much in the depiction of Dombey that graveled Powell—what he felt was the "gross libelling" and pillorying of a man who was Dickens's fellow philanthropist and ostensibly his friend, not to say Powell's uncle, for the entertainment of hundreds of thousands of readers at home and abroad. For Dickens had "achieved a fame not only gladly recognized wherever the English tongue was spoken," but a fame that "extended into France, Germany, Italy, and Holland" as well (Whipple, 394). And Ralph Waldo Emerson (201) observed, if hyperbolically, during his 1847 lecture at Manchester that "as for Dombey, sir, there is no land where paper exists to print on, where it is not found; no man who can read, that does not read it, and, if he cannot, he finds some charitable pair of eyes that can."

Powell himself, of course, had violated his uncle's trust, but he probably rationalized it as a private, not a public, act—one that struck Chapman only in his pocketbook, not in his honor and reputation. Chapman was still, as Dickens once put it about Augustus, his "bit of blood" who had taken him into his business, taught him the trade, rewarded him with high position, and who, despite Powell's years of clandestine embezzlement and forgery, had forgiven him his trespasses. And who in all likelihood had even arranged to get Powell out of the country so that he could escape prison or transportation.

This appears to be the explanation for Powell's turnabout in his attitude toward Dickens. For at the outset (Document 1) he had admired Dickens enormously for his comic and tragic power, his "noble spirit of Christian charity . . . in all appropriate places throughout [his] works," and who as an author could "touch pitch without soiling his fingers."

Dickens, of course, was aware that Chapman had not prosecuted Powell—among other reasons, to prevent the spread of the scandal. In this respect Chapman was successful, as the newspapers caught no wind of it. Hence, as appears below, Dickens's cap-in-hand request of Chapman to set forth Powell's criminal "history in the plainest possible terms," and hence Chapman's presumed refusal, as the Preface to the Cheap Edition of American Notes (1850), which was supposed to present the criminal history, contains no mention of Powell at all.

My Dear Sir

I believe Augustus will have shewn you (in an American Newspaper) a new proof of the villainy and unblushing falsehood of that execrable rascal Powell [see Document 23].

A reprint of my American Notes will be the next issue in my Cheap Edition, and will not occupy, in completing, more than a couple of months, I think. I hope you will see no objection to my instancing (in a new Preface) this fellow's easy connexion with an American Newspaper, as a striking proof of the justice of the estimation in which I hold that Press, and to my setting forth his history in the plainest possible terms. I think such an unmitigated villain should be denounced, and I know that it would go all over the States instantly.

Believe Me/Faithfully Yours Always/Charles Dickens

---

28. *22 October 1849: From a Letter to Lewis Gaylord Clark*

Charles Dickens

Since Chapman, among other reasons, wanted the Powell scandal kept quiet, he presumably requested Dickens to refrain from using his Preface to the Cheap Edition of American Notes *to expose it to all and sundry. Dickens, therefore, took another tack, for as he said—to Powell himself when they were on good terms—"When we doos go in, we plays to win Sir" (P, 4:106). He thus reviewed Powell's criminal history for Lewis Gaylord Clark, a great admirer of the novelist and editor/owner of the popular* Knickerbocker, *in the hope, no doubt, that Clark would publish it in his magazine. (Dickens later told Charles Kent, the editor of the London* Sun, *that he had "requested him [Clark] to publish that piece of information," Document 55.) In the process Dickens referred to Powell's latest confidence trick.*

That con occurred almost as soon as Powell arrived in New York in September 1849. He presented to a J. G. Body of New York a letter of introduction to George Veasey & Co., as well as two drafts upon that Quebec bank totaling £250. The letter of introduction and the drafts bore the name of John Allan, the junior partner of Chapman & Co., whose signature Powell had forged. Mr. Body, having no reason to suspect this bluff, prosperous-looking, and altogether plausible Englishman, might even have been pleased to help the London gentleman to £250. When Powell's fraud was discovered, he was arrested, but, as Mr. Body reported to John Allan, "We [had] no evidence of the forgery of your name, and he was discharged" (Documents 23 & 52).

Had there been such evidence, Powell could have been extradited, since, according to the treaty ratified by the United States and Great Britain in 1842, forgery was specified as one of six extraditable offences. However, extradition could take place only upon two conditions: when the crime was established by judicial inquiry and was common to both countries (Bedi, 78-79, 138). While the second condition was satisfied in the case of Powell, the first condition had not been met. In any event, it is doubtful that Chapman, who had suppressed the scandal, would want to revive it now by bringing his profligate nephew home to face charges.

Dickens, to indicate how much Powell had once admired him, alleges in the letter below that Powell had dedicated one of his plays to him. Dedicating books was a common practice: Dickens, for example, had dedicated Pickwick *to Talfourd,* Nickleby *to Macready,* Chuzzlewit *to Miss Coutts, and* Dombey *to the Marchioness of Normanby. Powell, too, dedicated his plays to various friends, but "none of his published plays is dedicated to Dickens" (P, 5:4). Carried away by polemics, Dickens had no doubt glorified a mere inscription in a Powell book into a dedication. In all likelihood the book was* The Blind Wife *(1842), as it was listed in the "Inventory of Books" at Dickens's Devonshire Terrace house (P, 4:711).*

Despite Dickens's promise to Clark that he would "certainly relate these facts [about Powell] myself in a Preface to the Cheap Edition of my American Notes, *which will appear . . . in some two or three months," he did not need to keep his word, as Clark in November (Document 32) proceeded to publish the facts for him.*

. . . But I have *another* piece of news for you. I am going to give you a serious caution respecting a man who has been, and possibly may yet be, in New York, and who I think very likely to have fallen in your way. You know my opinion of American newspapers generally. Therefore you will believe, when you come to the end of what I am going to tell you, that I am not surprised to learn from a brother of mine, that one of your newspapers (I think it is called the *New York Evening Post*) has been puffing a Mr. Thomas Powell, an English Literary Gentleman, and publishing a life of me by that eminent Individual, purporting to be a part of some forthcoming book, which is, from beginning to end, one intact and complete Lie. I think Mr. Powell a very likely kind of man indeed, to form a ready connexion with the American Press.

He is a Forger and a Thief. He was Managing Clerk to an eminent Merchant's House in the City of London, and during a series of years forged and altered cheques until he had defrauded them to the extent of Thousands upon Thousands of pounds. His robberies being discovered one day he took up his hat, went to a chemist's, bought some laudanum, walked off to a warm bath, and was found in it insensible. I don't know whether he took Laudanum enough to kill himself, but I should say he was careful to keep on the safe side. He was recovered, and forgiven by the gentleman he had robbed—dismissed, of course, but not prosecuted. They were tender of his wife and family. After some months['] endurance of the misery and shame of his position, he was taken up at Croydon (ten miles from London) for passing several forged cheques to divers tradespeople in that neighbourhood—was stated [by his solicitor] to the Magistrate[s] to be mad—and was actually confined for some time in a Lunatic Asylum, that the prosecutions against him might not go on. [Actually, Powell was not "taken up at Croydon" after some months but after more than two years.] From the Lunatic Asylum, he found his way to New York. He arrived there, with a forged letter of recommendation to credit, *purporting to come from a partner in the very house he robbed,* and drew two bills upon that gentleman (in New York) which, of course, have been protested and returned. The very same House, to whose moderation he is indebted for his not working in chains in Norfolk Island at this instant, is, of course, the object of his blackest ingratitude, and is libelled in all sorts of ways[!]—in his aforesaid life of me.

Before his character was discovered, he wrote some plays—one dedicated to me—by pushing which he got into the houses of certain Literary men, and among others into mine, where he once dined, I am sorry to say. I know his late employers well, and tell you this story with a full and complete personal knowledge of its truth in every particular. It is under-stated.

I shall certainly relate these facts myself in a Preface to the Cheap Edition of my American Notes, which will appear in a Serial Re-Issue of my books, in some two or three months. You are at liberty to make any use of this communication that you think proper. I am responsible for its truth, and think your American readers will do well to consider whom they trust to, sometimes.

Ever My Dear Clark Faithfully Yours,/Charles Dickens

---

29. *1 November 1849: From a Letter to William Parker Snow*

Charles Dickens

Snow, an Englishman who had gone to New York in 1849, had apparently written a flattering sketch of Dickens's life, a copy of which he now sent the novelist. Given Powell's recent essay on him, Dickens was pleased with the spirit of the sketch (never published) and said that it has "my cordial and grateful recognition." He added that there were errors in the sketch which he could not correct "because if I ever corrected my volunteer biographers, I should begin a labor which would only end, in all probability, with my life itself."

There was, nevertheless, one error that Dickens proceeded to correct: one referring to Powell. For he saw in Snow another agent, in addition to his friend Clark (Document 28), to expose Powell's criminality. He even told Snow that he was "at perfect liberty to make any use of this communication you please."

. . . Your allusion to an imposition practised on the New York public by one Mr. Thomas Powell, in the form of another life of me, renders it necessary for me to say that I have been made acquainted with its contents, and that it is, from first to last, an invention and a lie. But you will be the less surprised at this, perhaps, when I inform you that the life of this same Mr. Powell has been, for many years past, a course of forgery and theft. His history is perfectly well known to me, and to many other gentlemen now in London. He was a trusted clerk in a merchant's house for many years, and, for years, robbed his employers by innumerable acts of forgery and fraud. Being forgiven by them, when detected, he has (very naturally for such a man, as I think) libelled them ever since—even in the very composition to which I have just now referred. After being dismissed from their service, he was carried [more than two years later] before the Magistrates at Croydon, charged with passing forged cheques to a variety of tradespeople in that neighbourhood; and only escaped the punishment due to this offence by getting some friends who had known him in the days when he was supposed to be honest, to confine him in a lunatic asylum, where he actually remained for some time as a Madman, and whence he emigrated to New York to delight and enlighten the American Public as a distinguished literary character from England.

As he has obtained money in New York, on the strength of certain bills, drawn (and cashed, I believe) on the faith of a forged letter of credit from England; and as those bills have been returned protested, with a formal declaration that he is a swindler; I presume his literary and truthful course in America is already run,—the more especially as I have myself written these particulars to a friend [L. G. Clark] in that City. But in case he should be still administering to the intellectual gratification of the New York public, you are at perfect liberty to make any use of this communication you please.

---

30. *16 November 1849: Review of Thomas Powell's* The Living Authors of England *in the* New York Tribune

George Ripley

This critique, signed "R," was written by George Ripley, who typically signed his reviews in the Tribune *with that single initial.*

When fire ravaged Brook Farm, which Ripley had founded, Horace Greeley invited him to move his editorial quarters to the Tribune Building, for Greeley was also a champion of Fourierism. Among other things, Greeley had helped to found the North American Phalanx, the most scientifically planned of all the American experiments in Fourierism. At his new quarters Ripley continued putting out the weekly Harbinger, *his Fourierite journal. Upon its demise in February 1849, Ripley succeeded Margaret Fuller as literary critic of the* Tribune.

Ripley was incensed at Powell's treatment of Washington Irving, America's first international author and assuredly among the most revered of living Americans. For Powell had charged (in his sketch of John Forster in Living Authors of England*) that Irving was nothing more than an "agreeable essayist, and a very successful imitator of the level style of Addison and Pope"; that he had pillaged Forster's* Life and Adventures of Oliver Goldsmith *(1848) for his revised edition of Goldsmith (1849); and that his work suffered from "faded piracy, tame sentimentalism, and common-place suavity."*

It is rather an ominous fact, that a work professing to give a faithful portraiture of some of the most eminent living authors of Great Britain should be obliged to cross the Atlantic in order to find a publisher. The secret, however, is explained as soon as we open the volume. We have no special admiration of the English publishing houses, great or small, but we are certain that no one of them could consent for a moment to palm upon the world such a puny, puling, misshapen and monstrous literary production as the present work. We trust that it is no proof of the supremacy of the "almighty dollar" over the decencies of literature in this country, that it has induced a respectable house to lend it the sanction of their name.

Mr. Powell, we believe, is not altogether unknown as an author. He has written some pieces for the stage, which we are told are not without a certain kind of merit. But if we may judge from the flippant and foolish work before us, his poverty of qualification for passing judgment on the great writers of England is equaled only by the audacity of his presumption.

The staple of his book is a collection of flimsy gossip, stale anecdotes, and disgusting personalities and puerilities, which a vulgar hanger-on to the outskirts of literary society in England could easily pick up, and the most amusing of which—if that word can be applied to any of them—we have known to be related by second-rate travelers, till they are worn out by the nauseous repetition.—Mr. Powell, occasionally, attempts a higher flight. He sometimes ceases to describe the color of the hair and eyes of his victims, and ventures to pass judgment on their writings. His criticisms we scarcely need say are usually ludicrous and always worthless. The remarks which he appends to some of the noble quotations which fall within his reach are sickening specimens of what has been called "inspiration and water." We are unwilling to offend our readers by producing any instances of his unmitigated twaddle.

Mr. Powell's attack on our illustrious countryman Washington Irving is a graver character. We will not insult the admirable modesty of Mr. Irving by dwelling on this Billingsgate assault, but we cannot let it pass without a glance. It illustrates the tastes and manners of the author. We may learn from it his competency for the work he has volunteered. Besides, it is too rich an exhibition of the ass's kick at a living lion, not to afford us a smile, in relief of the dull stupidity which pervades the book. The criticism on Irving is a piece of altogether gratuitous impertinence. It is not promised on the title page. It is more than we bargained for. The Living Authors of America, Heaven save the mark! are announced as the subject of a future volume. We are treated to this delicious morsel on Irving as a stomachic before the feast.

Mr. Powell first informs us that W.(!) Irving holds a "false position in American Literature." But is that a reason why he should curtail his name of "its fair proportions." Mr. Powell then proceeds to favor us with the proof. "It is a complete fallacy to consider the author of the Sketch Book as anything beyond an agreeable essayist, and a very successful imitator of the level style of Addison and Pope." This is not the worst of the case. Mr. Powell has taken away the literary reputation of W. Irving; he must now destroy his moral character. Insatiate archer! "Mr. Irving has just given to the world" (in his Life of Goldsmith) "so glaring an instance of unscrupulous appropriation of the labor of another, that it is utterly impossible to avoid arraigning the offender" as sharing in the "piracy of American publishers, which has been such a favorite topic for indignant vituperation."

A more outrageous calumny was never put forth by the father of lies.

Perhaps there may be some apology for Mr. Irving. He does not know how to write. He is a villain by reason of mental imbecility. For Mr. Powell condescends further to inform us that his book is made up of "faded piracy, tame sentimentalism, and common-place suavity." What he means by "faded piracy," is somewhat doubtful. Black is the orthodox color for piracy; when faded we presume it becomes "whity-brown." Whether it is less of a crime in that case, in Mr. Powell's estimation, we will not venture to say.

Our readers may be able to form some judgment of the pretensions of this scurrilous volume. We do not accept the vulgarity of the source as an atonement for the shamefulness of the outrage. If the book had stood by itself, we might have let it decay in its own infamy. But as it has been indorsed by some of our contemporaries, (thoughtlessly, we have no doubt,) we have felt bound to hold up the worthless paper to the light. Its lively anecdote has been claimed as its passport into good company. We should as soon select a harridan for the society of our daughters on account of a voluble tongue.

R.

---

31. *16 November 1849: A Parody of Thomas Powell's* Living Authors of England

New York Evening Mirror

The Mirror *publishes a crude travesty of Powell's book under the head, "Dead Authors of England" by Thomas Towel, which is dedicated "To the gentlewoman who taught me the art of humbugging." An editorial disclaimer protested that the "work is not by Thomas Powell, Esq., the vilifier of Dicken[s], &c., &c."*

The authors chosen by "Thomas Towel" were Wordsworth, Shakespeare, Byron, Lindley Murray, and Milton. The treatment of Wordsworth is typical of the way the parodist handled the other four authors.

William Wordsworth.—This individual, the son of his mother, was born. He has written verses, and was at one time *poet laureat* [*sic*]. *I* never thought much of him, and *whenever* we dined together, I always said to Bill (I called him by his Christian name,) what *I* thought of him. He seemed pleased with my remarks, and said he would endeavor to improve, but *I* regret to state that he has not amended his verses. As a specimen I quote the following seven hundred lines.

(Here follows the quotation, which we must omit.—Editors.)

Mr. Wordsworth is not dead, (although I have so classed him,) and when I last received a note from him, he begged me to speak favorably of him; at the same time he enclosed a one pound note as a token of friendship. For further particulars of Mr. W. I must refer you, "very kind reader," to your imagination—a source whence I draw most of my facts.

---

32. *20 November 1849: "A Scoundrel Branded"*

Lewis Gaylord Clark in the New York Tribune

As Dickens had hoped, Clark took up Dickens's vendetta against Powell and sent a letter to New York newspapers, some of which, like the Evening Mirror, *the* Herald, *and the* Tribune, *published it. Clark's letter, which contained an extract from Dickens's letter exposing Thomas Powell, was also "copied extensively in the papers through the Union" (Document 44).*

"Puffer Hopkins" refers to Cornelius Mathews, the American author of The Career of Puffer Hopkins. *Powell, it appears, had been introduced by Evert Duyckinck to Mathews's novel which had been published serially (1841-42) in* Arcturus, *a magazine co-edited by Duyckinck and Mathews, his* ami de coeur.

Mathews had long been a personal target of Clark. As Duyckinck charged in a counter-blast at Clark: "During eight years the Knickerbocker Magazine has published various attacks upon Mr. Mathews and his writings, with a malignity and pertinacity which once induced the Tribune *to call loudly for the private reasons which instigated such a course. It has misrepresented and traduced him in many ways by misstatements, by partial quotations, by hints and innuendos and all the machinery which a little mind knows so well to employ for its ends. . . . His writings have been systematically depreciated; and according to a cheap and favorite argument with this journal, it has been suggested that he is out of his mind. . . . The Knickerbocker should be put into Coventry by the respectable press" (Moss, 103-4).*

To the Editors of The Tribune:

Knickerbocker Sanctum, Nov. 17, 1849

Gentlemen: I send you an extract from a letter received by me from Mr. Charles Dickens, by the last English steamer. It strikes me as but just to Mr. Dickens, as well as to our community, that the facts which it sets forth should be made public. The volume of this Mr. Powell, to which *The Tribune* has assisted to give the unenviable notoriety [Document 30], and which it would have secured for itself, had it been as widely read as your journal, is no doubt as *authentic* in respect of other English writers mentioned in its pages as it is in relation to Mr. Dickens. It is to be hoped that the circumstance of the book's not being at all reliable in its accounts of persons, may not lessen the value of its critical opinions! It may still be true (may it not?) that the fire of Mr. Dickens's genius pales before the intellectual sun of "Puffer Hopkins," from whom Boz is charged to have plagiarized some of his best scenes; and that few writers equal 'Mr. W. Irving' in 'tame sentimentalism,' 'faded piracy,' and 'flimsy commonplace.'

Yours Faithfully,/L. Gaylord Clark

[Here Clark quoted the extract about Powell from Dickens's letter of 22 October 1849 (Document 28) in its entirety, except for expurgating two passages. The first passage, which is fragmentary, is: "You know my opinion of American newspapers generally. Therefore you will believe, when you come to the end of what I am going to tell you, that I am not surprised to learn"; the second: "I shall certainly relate these facts myself in a Preface to the Cheap Edition of my American Notes, which will appear in a Serial Re-Issue of my books, in some two or three months."]

---

33. *20 November 1849: "Charles Dickens and the American Press"*

William Cullen Bryant in the New York Evening Post

Bryant, who took great pride in his integrity and in the honorable reputation of his newspaper, was provoked at Dickens's accusation that a forger and thief like Thomas Powell "was a very likely kind of man, indeed, to form a ready connection with the American Press." Bryant was incensed still more at Greeley and Clark because the Tribune, *in printing Dickens's letter, did not answer the insult and because Clark, though himself a member of the press, seemed to take the insult as a compliment.*

Bryant added that he had no compunction about Powell's exposure of Dickens, as the novelist had himself "made so free with the personal characters of men now living." This charge of Bryant's was an oft-repeated one, for Dickens did not always pulp his acquaintance before serving them up so that, as Fanny Trollope put it, the pig would not be recognized in the sausage. That reiterated charge, however, did nothing to deter Dickens from modeling characters on living individuals, among them his friends John Forster (Podsnap) and Leigh Hunt (Skimpole), for instance. Not a fault perhaps: romans à clef *are a commonplace; and* now, *of course, it does not much matter. But* then, *while Dickens was having, to use Pugh's phrase, "high-spirited fun" caricaturing people, it was wormwood for those models. In 1857 Powell had called the Skimpole character "the most skilful of Dickens's malignant caricatures"* (Chit-Chat, *322). The cruelest of such cases involved a grotesquely deformed dwarf, Dickens's neighbor Mrs. Seymour Hill, upon whom he modeled Mrs. Mowcher* (David Copperfield*). "I have suffered long and much," she complained to Dickens, "from my personal deformities but never before at the hands of a Man so highly gifted as Charles Dickens and hitherto considered as a Christian and Friend to his fellow Creatures. . . . Tell me how I have deserved your anger" (P, 5:674n).*

A few days later Dickens received a letter from Mrs. Hill's solicitor threatening a libel suit, and Dickens, attempting to underplay the damage, promised "to repair the uneasiness" he had "unintentionally caused her" by rehabilitating Mrs. Mowcher's character as soon as the plot of the novel permitted (P, 5:677).

We republish from the *Tribune* of this morning a letter from L. G. Clark, Editor of the Knickerbocker, introducing another from Charles Dickens, respecting the author of a book recently published in this country, under the title of "Living Authors of England." It is due to the cause of truth, that the real character of one who has made so free with the personal characters of men now living, should be exposed, but there is one passage in Mr. Dickens's letter which we cannot allow to pass without some notice. He says:

"I think Mr. Powell a very likely man, indeed, to form a ready connection with the American press. He is a forger and a thief."

That any daily paper in publishing this letter, manifestly written for publication, should, as the Tribune has done, silently accept the insult it casts upon the whole American press without exception, is what we can only account for by supposing that the import of its language escaped notice; but that Mr. Clark, the editor of one of our periodicals, should have sent it to be published with as much alacrity as if the abuse bestowed upon himself and the rest of his class was a compliment, is what we cannot account for at all.

Mr. Dickens, it seems from his own letter, has been on terms of some intimacy with Mr. Powell. Powell wrote a play, which he dedicated to Dickens, was received as a visitor at his house, and invited to his table. Suppose it were to be said, by way of retort, "Mr. Powell is a very likely man indeed to form a *ready* connection with Mr. Dickens; he is a forger and a thief." The occasion for the remark would certainly be as fair in this case as in the other.

Mr. Powell, however, has not, that we heard of, formed any connection with the American press, farther than to publish his book. With the Evening Post he never had any connection whatever, nor has he ever been "puffed" in our sheet. The portion of the forth-coming work which we published [Document 22] was sent us by the respectable house of D. Appleton & Co., and we published only a part of what related to Dickens. It made a readable article enough; and if its facts were not accurate, that was a matter of which we could have no suspicion. Mr. Dickens, though the phraseology of his letter would lead one to suppose he had never read it, calls it "one intact and complete lie."

What an "intact lie" may be, we cannot explain; but the whole letter indicates some confusion of ideas at the time it was penned, which perhaps ought to be received as some extenuation of its insolence. As to the criticisms in the biography we published, if they were not to Mr. Dickens's taste, we do not see why he should take his revenge on the whole American press. On such questions as the merits of a contemporary novelist, people will differ very widely, and there is no such thing as reducing their opinions to an orthodox standard.

Perhaps we have taken more notice of this matter than our readers will think it deserves, but the grossness of the assault must be our excuse.

[With minor variants, Clark's letter, which included Dickens's (Document 32) followed this introduction.]

---

34. *23 November 1849: L. Gaylord Clark Replies to William Cullen Bryant*

New York Tribune

Clark publishes his reply to Bryant's recriminations (Document 33), a reply that also appeared in the Boston Evening Transcript *on 26 November and no doubt elsewhere.*

"Puffer Hopkins" was the nickname Clark had attached to Cornelius Mathews (Headnote to Document 32).

To the Editors of The Tribune:

Gentlemen—A writer in the *Evening Post* complains of the undue 'alacrity' with which I sent to your press the exposé by Mr. Dickens, of the character of Mr. Thomas Powell, the concocter of 'The Living Authors of England.' The letter would first have appeared in the *Knickerbocker,* for December, but that I was led to the belief by certain circumstances, that its publication was a necessary caution to the community.

The *Evening Post* published the extract entire from the letter of Mr. Dickens, and that speaks for itself. Meantime, probability *rather* favors the conclusion, that when a newly-arrived Englishman, of the stamp of Mr. Powell, after a stay of some three months in New-York, is enabled to publish from an American press a book such as his, he may be said to have formed a somewhat ready connection with that press.

The respectable and popular publishers of 'The Living Authors of England' informed me more than two weeks since that they much regretted having been persuaded to publish Powell's work; and that if a second edition were demanded in a week they should not issue it. And who, leaving out of question the personal calumnies, would desire to stand god-father to a book whose critical discrimination (Heaven save the mark!) places the 'genius' of the author of 'Puffer Hopkins' on a par with that of Dickens and which assigns to Washington Irving the position of a 'tame,' 'overrated,' 'common-place' writer, who is 'a gross plagiarist' withal, and 'struts like a daw in peacock's feathers!'

The writer in the *Post,* alluding to the 'criticism' in the 'Living Authors' remarks:

On such questions as the merits of a contemporary novelist, people will differ very widely, and there is no such thing as reducing their opinions to an orthodox standard.

'Contemporary novelist!!' that was Puffer's voice, if ever Puffer spoke!

But, gentlemen, I've 'said all my say' now; and must attend to my own [Editor's] 'Table,' instead of laying any more hasty slips upon yours.

Faithfully Yours,/L. Gaylord Clark

---

35. *21 November 1849: "A Literary Humbug Exposed"*

Boston Evening Transcript

The Transcript, *like many another journal, was offended by Powell's charge in his* Living Authors of England *that Dickens and Irving were plagiaristic, the former from Cornelius Mathews ("Puffer Hopkins"), the latter from John Forster.*

A Literary Humbug Exposed. A few weeks since the Messrs. Appleton of New York published a volume entitled "The Living Authors of England, by Thomas Powell." It was well spoken of in the New York Literary World [Document 25] and other journals, and contained a good deal of cockney-ish gossip, new to Americans, in regard to some of the literary celebrities of the day. Although the style was not far above the calibre of a discharged valet, yet it indicated a smattering acquaintance with modern English literature, not unfitted to impose upon the superficial reader.

There were two passages in this book, in which the charlatanism and malicious motive of the author were signally displayed. One was an attempt to persuade the American public that Mr. Charles Dickens had pilfered some of his best things from the American author of "Puffer Hopkins!" The preposterousness of such a charge could only be sufficiently appreciated in the circle where that book and its author were known. It was exposed with well-merited ridicule in the New York Mirror and other journals.

The second *bêtise* [absurdity] in Mr. Powell's book was an impudent though imbecile attempt to soil the reputation of

Washington Irving with his countrymen. This gifted writer and most estimable man was accused, like Dickens, of plagiarism. We were also told by his Cockney critic, that "tame sentimentalism," "faded piracy" and "flimsy commonplace" were the characteristics of Mr. Irving's style. Many more insolent things were said of him, all implying that Mr. Irving had omitted to invite this terrible Mr. Powell to dinner.

Having disposed of the "Living Authors of England," we were told that Mr. Powell was turning his attention to those of the United States, and that a volume might be soon expected from his pen, giving to each his true niche in the temple of fame or consigning him, like Irving, to condemnation and oblivion. But unhappily for the critical career of Mr. Powell in America, Mr. Charles Dickens, like a remorseless Fate, has stepped in with his shears to slit the slender thread of his literary life. In the Tribune of yesterday we find the following extract from a letter from Mr. Dickens to Lewis Gaylord Clark of the Knickerbocker Magazine, received by the last steamer, in which the literary pretensions of Mr. Powell are disposed of in a very summary and unequivocal manner. In communicating this extract to the public, Mr. Clark says: "It strikes me as but just to Mr. Dickens, as well as to our community, that the facts which it sets forth should be made public." Here it is; and we can think of but one consolation for Mr. Powell after reading it,—let him devote himself once more to the pages of "Puffer Hopkins!"

[Here follows Dickens's letter to Clark (Document 28).]

---

36. *22 November 1849: Thomas Powell's Attorney Threatens a Lawsuit Against Hiram Fuller and Fuller's Reply*

New York Evening Mirror

In an undated letter Powell had written to Evert Duyckinck: "My lawyer [J. L. White] will call on you tomorrow and ask you a few questions, as I will do nothing final *without your advice. You can answer him without hesitation, but I am determined . . . to expose the malice of two or three persons."*

The letter Powell's attorney refers to in the document below is the one which disseminated Dickens's letter exposing Powell's criminal history (Document 32).

The "Byron case" that Fuller mentions involved a major—sometimes colonel—Byron, who claimed to be the son of Lord Byron and a Countess De Luna of Spain, who forged and published The Inedited Works of Lord Byron *(1849) in New York. When Fuller in his newspaper denounced Byron as an "arrant humbug," Byron filed a libel suit against him, demanding five thousand dollars in damages. The verdict went against the major, who passed himself off as George Gordon De Luna Byron (Ehrsam, 67, 68, 74).*

We received yesterday the following legal *billet-doux* [love letter]:—

New York, Nov. 21st, 1849.

Hiram Fuller, Esq:—

Sir:—Mr. Thomas Powell has instructed me to commence suit against you, as Editor of the Mirror, for the publication of a letter purporting to be written by Mr. Charles Dickens, and charging on Mr. P. the commission of offences of an aggravated character.

Perhaps you had better see Mr. Powell and settle the matter with him. For this purpose I will postpone proceedings for a day or two.

Yours, &c. J. L. White,
No. 14, Wall-street.

Now as we have only offended in common with the *Tribune*, the *Evening Post*, the *Newark Daily Advertiser*, the *Boston Transcript*, and others "too numerous to mention," we trust that all the libellers may be lumped and tried together. We already have the *Byron case* on our hands, and it is hardly handsome to make us the "scape goat" of the universal Press.—Ed. Mirror.

---

37. *23 November 1849: Letter in the New York Evening Post*

Thomas Powell

Under his own name, not his lawyer's this time, Powell sends a letter to various New York papers, including the Evening Mirror, *the* Morning Express, *and the* Evening Post. *In that letter he threatens to bring further actions for libel (Document 36) and promises to refute, in a Preface to his forthcoming book (*The

Living Authors of America), *the charges Dickens preferred against him.*

Powell's refutation did not appear, perhaps because his publisher, Stringer & Townsend, did not want to risk becoming embroiled in one or more libel suits. Instead, Powell, during the course of the book, mentioned Dickens twice (20, 295), once to praise him for his comic treatment of the rival editors of Eatanswill in Pickwick, *the other to criticize his "absurd distortions" and "gross caricature."*

Mr. Dickens and Mr. Powell.—The following note from Mr. Powell appears in the Express of this morning. It appears, by the Mirror of last evening, that legal proceedings have been instituted by Mr. Powell against the editor of that journal, for the republication of Mr. Dickens's late letter to Mr. Clark:

To the Public

To the Editor of the Express:—

Sir: I have seen in several of the public papers a letter purporting to be written by L. Gaylord Clark, introducing an extract from one which he represents to have received from Mr. Charles Dickens.

With reference to the statements against me, contained therein, they are false and scandalous, and I must request the public to suspend their judgment until the matter is brought before a legal tribunal, steps for which purpose having already been taken.

In the preface to my forthcoming volume which will be published in a few days, I shall effectually refute, to the satisfaction of the American Public, the outrageous calumnies of Mr. Charles Dickens, to which, perhaps, he may have been provoked by my recent work entitled "The Living Authors of England."

Nov. 21st, 1849. Respectfully,/Thomas Powell

---

38. *24 November 1849: "Police Intelligence: Literary War and Charge of Libel"*

New York Herald

As he had promised (Document 37), Thomas Powell brought a charge of criminal libel against Lewis Gaylord Clark before a

New York Justice, who issued a warrant for Clark's arrest to answer to the charge and who set bail at $500, according to the Police Court Docket Book. That was no trivial amount, as it was more than half the average annual salary earned by a professor. Even during the Civil War, a man, drafted into the Union Army for a three-year term, could avoid military service by paying $300 for a substitute, a sum constituting about two-thirds of a workingman's annual income.

A sensational article like the one below was copied throughout the country. On 27 November, for instance, the Boston Evening Transcript *copied it, with acknowledgment, from the* Herald.

Literary War—Charge of Libel—Yesterday, Mr. Thomas Powell appeared before Justice Mountfort, at the Police Court, and complained that a gross libel had been perpetrated upon his good fame, and referred the magistrate to a portion of a letter purporting to be written by Charles Dickens, from London, to Mr. L. Gaylord Clark, editor of the *Knickerbocker*, in this city, wherein it was stated that Mr. Powell was a forger and a thief, together with other hard and violent language used towards Mr. Powell, tending to defame the moral standing of Mr. Powell in the eyes of the public. The extract or portion of this letter containing the libellous matter complained of was published in the *Tribune*, of the 20th instant, under the signature of Mr. Clark, and headed "A Scoundrel Branded" [Document 32]. The magistrate, on reading the article alleged to be libellous, took the affidavit of Mr. Powell, and a warrant was issued for the arrest of Mr. Clark, to answer the charge.

---

39. *25 November 1849: "Terrible Row Among the Literati"*

James Gordon Bennett in the New York Herald

Bennett amplifies the Herald *report (Document 38), explaining that Powell had initiated a* criminal *suit for libel against Lewis Gaylord Clark and a* civil *suit for libel against Hiram Fuller, editor of the* New York Mirror, *and Horace Greeley, the editor, and Thomas McElrath, the publisher, of the* New York Tribune.

To commence a criminal prosecution the complainant's charge is submitted to the District Attorney. The proceeding, if undertaken, is then introduced in the name of the People on the complaint of the plaintiff. A statement of charges specifies the breach of peace that has occurred in consequence of the offense, the criminal statutes allegedly violated, and the punishment provided in the statutes: a prison term and possibly a fine, but no monetary damages to the complainant. The defendant is then haled before a magistrate, who decides upon the testimony heard whether to hold him for the Grand Jury. If so decided, the defendant must post bail to assure his appearance before the Grand Jury or else be jailed. Should the Grand Jury find sufficient prima facie evidence to warrant an indictment, the defendant is brought before a court to plead.

A civil suit has the advantage over a criminal prosecution in that a far lesser degree of guilt need be proved. As one lawyer put it, a criminal prosecution requires 99 per cent certainty of guilt to be established, since a prison sentence and a fine may be the result, whereas a civil action requires only 51 per cent certainty of guilt, since only money is involved.

"Naval Storekeeper" was Bennett's term of contempt for Hiram Fuller, editor of the New York Mirror, *who in 1848 had accepted the New York position of quartermaster, a sinecure awarded him for being among the first to have discerned presidential qualities in General Zackery Taylor. Or, as Lewis Gaylord Clark put it, "Our friend Mr. Fuller finds leisure . . . to attend to the duties of the honorable and lucrative station which he holds under 'Uncle Samuel,' and to edit his . . . spritely and most readable journal."*

Terrible Row among the Literati.—Libels and Libel Suits.—A terrible, but amusing row, or explosion, has taken place among some of the small *literati* on both sides of the great waters, that almost equals, in piquancy, the explosion which recently took place between the cabinet, at Washington, and the villainous New York *Herald*, of this city.

Mr. Clark, of the *Knickerbocker Magazine,* corresponds with Dickens, the English novelist. After the arrival of the mail one day, Clark runs to Greeley, of the *Tribune*, and publishes an extract of a letter from Dickens, charging a Mr. Powell, another literary man of this city, of being guilty of forgery, or theft, and of a whole host of other villainies. Mr. Powell immediately commenced prosecutions against all those who published such terrible and shocking charges in this country. Accordingly, a criminal indictment is about to be got up against Clark, for the purpose, if what he says is false, of sending him to the penitentiary. A similar process is about to be commenced against the Naval Storekeeper for publishing Dickens' letter; and a prosecution for damages will be commenced against Greeley & McElrath, as it will punish them more to take money out of their purse, than to send them to the penitentiary, or anywhere else.

---

40. ***26 November 1849: "Libel Complaint"***

New York Tribune

The Tribune *confirms that Thomas Powell had filed a criminal libel complaint against Lewis Gaylord Clark and that a warrant had been issued for his arrest.*

Libel Complaint.—A complaint was . . . preferred before Justice Mountfort, by Thomas Powell, against Mr. L. Gaylord Clark, editor of the *Knickerbocker Magazine*, charging him with having caused to be published in *The Tribune* of the 20th inst. an article headed, "A Scoundrel Branded" [Document 32] which contains, as is alleged, a gross libel upon Powell's character, and is calculated to injure him in his vocation as a writer and publisher. A warrant [for Clark's arrest] has been issued.

---

41. ***26 November 1849: "Frightful Row Among the Literati—A Splendid Prospect for Blackwell's Island"***

James Gordon Bennett in the New York Herald

This article is marked by Bennett's antic humor and mad invention that characterized his style, charmed his readers, and won his Herald *one of the largest circulations in the world.*

"Puffer Hopkins" was Cornelius Mathews's nickname.

"Naval Storekeeper" refers to Hiram Fuller of the New York Mirror.

Blackwell's Island was the site of a lunatic asylum and a prison and had recently been put under the "Ten Governor System" to which Bennett refers.

Buntline, the pseudonym of Edward Zane Carroll Judson, editor of the magazine, Ned Buntline's Own, *was serving a year's sentence at Blackwell's for leading a mob in June 1849 against William Charles Macready (the great English tragedian and Dickens's dearest friend) in the Astor Place Riot.*

*Bennett's remarks about Dickens's speculations in railroads cannot be substantiated. The novelist, by his own acknowledgment made in June 1848, would never be poor again. "Within these three years or so," he wrote, I "have worked back half my copyrights . . . and have got, by some few thousand pounds . . . ahead of the world." And he added: "*Dombey *has been the greatest success I have ever achieved" (P, 5:341), as indeed it was, averaging more than twenty-five thousand copies of its nineteen installments, to say nothing of the hardback edition that appeared in April 1848. Moreover, in 1844 Dickens had been induced by Bradbury & Evans to leave Chapman & Hall. One inducement was that, upon an interest-free advance of £2800, he assign them a fourth share in whatever he might write during the next eight years. Another was a provision that if Dickens undertook to edit a periodical for them, even as a part-time editor or author, his "proprietorship of copyright and profits [apart from salary] was to be two-thirds" (Forster, 1:300).* Dombey *was the first of the Dickens novels to be published by Bradbury & Evans. Lest these figures mean little, it should be recalled that Dickens bought the Gad's Hill mansion, if somewhat in disrepair, for under £1,790.*

Given his new-found wealth, it would be surprising, then, if Dickens had not invested in railroad stock. In recent years he had briefly edited the Daily News, *a paper launched on a sea of railway advertising and capital generated by railway speculation. Of Joseph Paxton, a major backer of the* Daily News, *Dickens noted somewhat enviously, "he has command of every railway and railway influence in England and abroad except the Great Western; and he is in it, heart and purse" (P, 4:411). Also, at least half of American railroad paper had been bought up by English investors, including William Gladstone, John Bright, William Peel, Richard Cobden, and Samuel Cunard of steamship fame. As the American writer Caroline Kirkland (2:307-08) observed when in England: "The English . . . can only get three or four per cent. for money at home . . . [but] ten or twenty from us."*

If Powell, a born confidence man, had indeed involved Dickens in railway speculation to their financial loss (and certainly the destructive nature of railroad construction is an important element in Dombey*), Dickens would hardly have wanted others to know he had been victimized. Did Bennett's investigators learn about Dickens's alleged railway speculations from Powell, if indeed they did? The only outright implausibility in Bennett's report is that Thomas Chapman would rely on his nephew, if also his office manager, for financial advice when his associates were insurance brokers, bankers, and industrialists, and his firm was in the heart of London's financial district.*

A great sensation was created in our literary circles, a few days ago, by the publication of a most singular and alarming correspondence in the *New York Tribune,* and republished in the *Mirror* and other journals, as follows:

[Here Bennett reprints the whole of "A Scoundrel Branded," Document 32.]

This publication has led to a criminal prosecution against Mr. Clark, and all parties concerned in this city; and the affair has created so much anxiety and curiosity to know the meaning of all this, that we have undertaken, with great labor, and a vast outlay of money, to gather up the basis of this mysterious business.

A few years ago, Mr. Thomas Powell was a confidential clerk in a commercial house in London. Having a *penchant* for literary subjects, he sought the society of literary men, and was particularly happy in making the acquaintance of Dickens and his set, and other literary cliques; just as our amateurs plume themselves on getting into the Puffer Hopkins and balderdash cliques of this metropolis. About this time, the railway speculations commenced in England. Mr. Powell's employer thought that money was to be made in that line, and finding his clerk possessed of tact and capacity for the business, made him his confidential agent in the buying and selling of stocks, giving him the use of his name in signing drafts, checks, acceptances; etc. For a short time, everything went on swimmingly. [George] Hudson, the railway king, and all his agents, rolled in wealth. The California gold mines were mere moonshine, compared with the golden profits of their splendid operations. The fever was contagious, like the California [gold rush], and everybody that had a few thousands, or a few shillings to spare, invested the amount in railway shares. Mr. Dickens was seized with the fever. He wished to make money a little faster than by the drudgery of writing novels at a stated salary. He wished to flourish at the West End, and to roll in his carriage among the swells of Piccadilly and Hyde Park. Powell was the very man; and through his advice, Mr. Dickens put in for his share of the railway profits. But the thing turned out another South Sea bubble—it exploded, and in the revulsion evaporated like mist in the morning air. Ruin and bankruptcy followed close behind. The speculators turned upon each other, like snarling dogs; criminations and recriminations, and the most outrageous confessions, succeeded—just as we have often seen in Wall street, or in the late explosion of the State Bank of Morris. Norton accuses Thompson of being a rogue, and Thompson accuses Norton of being exactly the same thing, while the public have their suspicions that they are both telling the truth.

With the railway explosion, all hands were diddled, Powell's employers were tricked, Dickens was cheated, and Powell was ruined—the railroad king and his satellites, the speculators and the subscribers, fell together in the crash, like Nicholas Biddle, Watson Webb, the banks, and their victims, in 1837. Powell escaped to this country, and for a livelihood, commenced writing the book entitled "The Living Authors of England," of which the Appletons are the publishers. These sketches are small gossip, which don't amount to much; but they appear to have hit the sensitive feelings of Dickens, who, since his brilliant reception by our codfish aristocracy [in 1842], and the honors of the "Boz ball," has become exceedingly consequential and exclusive. He writes to Mr. Clark, (a literary man, with a good deal of extra superfine common sense,) his complaints and charges against Mr. Powell. Mr. Clark, of course, could not keep a letter from Dickens from the knowledge of the world, and so he forthwith publishes it, with a flourish of trumpets and kettle drums, in the *Tribune*. The *Mirror* and some other papers, with as little remorse or delicacy, take up the echo of "a scoundrel branded," and republish the correspondence without qualification or apology. Powell was thunderstruck, cut up, knocked down, trampled upon. No one could suppose that philosopher Greeley would brand "a man a scoundrel" unless the fact were so. But Powell soon recovered from the shock; and now comes the reaction.

Civil and criminal suits are to be instituted against the offending parties—Gaylord Clark, Horace Greeley, Hiram Fuller, the Naval Storekeeper, and all others concerned in the publication with a malicious intent. The trial will require the proofs, the facts, the tangible legal evidence, to support the accusations of Mr. Dickens. His mere unsupported declarations will simply amount to a libel. What then follows if Powell convicts these parties of this offence? We tremble to mention it. The philosopher Greeley, the financier McElrath [publisher of the *Tribune*], Mr. Clark, the literary man—the American Dickens [Cornelius Mathews]—and Hiram Fuller, the Naval Storekeeper, may all possibly become the boon companions of Ned Buntline before the next summer is over. The muses, the Fourierites, and the Naval Storekeeper, will have to go to Blackwell's Island, and probably work in the shoe shop at that place. What a galaxy of stars will be there! We shall look with most intense anxiety to the conclusion of this affair. Meantime, let the ten governors make all needful preparations for the proper reception of these distinguished guests on Blackwell's Island, if need be. Everybody will now want to read Powell's book. Appletons are the publishers. Go and buy it.

---

42. *27 November 1849: Hiram Fuller on Thomas Powell's Impending Libel Suit*

New York Evening Mirror

Fuller reports below that Powell had not yet filed a libel suit against him. That suit, however, would commence on 1 December 1849 (Documents 49 & 61).

The "other case" involving Fuller and a Major (or Colonel) Byron is explained in the Headnote to Document 36.

Fuller's abuse by the New York Herald *is explained in the Headnote to Document 39.*

In reply to numerous enquiries, we will state that no libel suit has yet been commenced against us for re-publishing, in common with our cotemporaries, the letter of Mr. Dickens, which originally appeared in the *Tribune*, touching one Thomas Powell. And in regard to the "other case," in which a correspondent volunteers some important testimony, we do not know *when* the evidence will be wanted, as the spurious Byron rather "hangs fire." So our cotemporaries need not waste their sympathies upon us at present; for, so long as we are hated only by humbugs, and abused by the New York *Herald*, we may consider ourselves more entitled to congratulation than condolence.

---

43. *26 November 1849: From a Letter to Richard Bentley*

Charles Dickens

Dickens was apprehensive that Bentley might republish Powell's Living Authors of England *in England and that its critique of him would circulate in his own country, thereby affecting his reputation and the sales of what he liked to call the "property." Dickens therefore proceeds to inform Bentley that in such an event he would expose Powell's criminal history to British readers in order to block sales of the book.*

That Bentley might have been interested in bringing out Living Authors *was plausible (though the advertisement Dickens mentions has not been found), for he had published two of Powell's books:* Tales from Boccaccio *(1846) and* Florentine Tales *(1847), an inscribed copy of which Powell presented to Thomas Chapman for having forgiven him his felonious trespasses. Though Bentley did not republish* Living Authors, *the English publishers, Partridge & Oakey, did so in 1851, though in an abbreviated edition and with a different title (Headnote to Document 67). Except for one sentence being eliminated, Powell's critique of Dickens remained intact.*

Early in his career (1837-39), Dickens had worked for Bentley, editing Bentley's Miscellany *and publishing* Oliver Twist *in it.*

Dickens's remark that he had sent particulars about Powell to America has reference to his letter to Clark (Document 28).

I observe that you advertize for republication in this country, a book recently published in America by one Mr. Thomas Powell, called The Living Authors of England.

I feel quite sure that you don't know Mr. Thomas Powell, and that you must be wholly unacquainted with his history—of which I have felt it necessary to send to America, some particulars. I think that after the receipt of this, you will not republish his book without further and careful enquiry. But I beg to say that if it be republished here by any one, I shall immediately publish my knowledge of Mr. Thomas Powell, which is of a rather startling and quite conclusive character.

I am Dear Sir/Faithfully Yours/Charles Dickens

---

44. *27 & 28 November 1849: "To the Press and the Public"*

Cornelius Mathews in the Tribune and Evening Post

Mathews replies to Lewis Gaylord Clark, whose "A Scoundrel Branded" was copied by newspapers throughout America. Why Mathews called Clark a malignant and persevering libeler is explained in the Headnote to Document 32.

In this instance Clark had been provoked by Powell's attempt in Living Authors of England *(Document 22) to demonstrate that Mathews's humor was superior to Dickens's and by Powell's implication that Dickens was imitative of Mathews. As Clark put it sarcastically in "A Scoundrel Branded": "The fire of Mr. Dickens's genius pales before the intellectual sun of 'Puffer Hopkins,' from whom Boz is charged to have plagiarized some of his best scenes."*

The Tribune *published Mathews's letter on the twenty-seventh with its initial paragraph excised. The document below is drawn from the* Evening Post *of the twenty-eighth.*

Gentlemen—Satisfied that the publication in the *Tribune, Evening Post,* and other journals of the card of "L. Gaylord Clark" has created an injurious impression, I have felt compelled to place on record a distinct protest in the enclosed card, to which I must ask of you to give the same publicity in your columns as to the original injury.

Respectfully, your ob't serv't,/Cornelius Mathews

To the Press and the Public.—It is with great pain and reluctance that I present myself before the Public on a purely personal question. The readers of newspapers will bear witness that I have sat down silently for years under assaults and misrepresentations more gross, more constant and unprovoked than any other person, whatever his profession or pursuit, in this country—and that, too, when I had in my hands at all times ample means to meet at any moment and put to shame such outrages. I have studiously avoided any recognition of these, partly from contempt, partly from indifference, but most of all from the consciousness of a blameless course, and a firm reliance on the final justice of the People. But, when I see an audacious attempt made by a malignant and persevering libeller, as a crowning effort of an eight-years' career of malice and mendacity against me, to couple my name with charges of an infamous nature, affecting the character of a third party, with which I am in no way concerned, I am compelled sorely against self-respect to break this long silence and to pronounce that assailant openly and before the world a coward and a slanderer. I refer to an article signed "L. Gaylord Clark," lately published in *The New-York Tribune*, and copied extensively in the papers through the Union, in which I am introduced and held up to scoffing and contempt in connection with criminal accusations against the author of the work lately issued, entitled "The Living Authors of England," simply because the writer of that work has thought proper to "compliment" me, an American author, in its pages. Such introduction and reference to me, as any fair-judging man must see, is wanton and impertinent, and purely an effort of low malice designing to avail itself of an opportunity to send my name through the country in a degrading connection. If there be any candor, manhood, or sense of fair-dealing in the American Press, I ask of such as have employed that card to brand it, by publishing this, my public protest, against the injury, as dastardly, wholly unprovoked, and as the most impudent contrivance of persevering malice ever witnessed in the annals of literary criticism, to gratify its unworthy promptings.

My reputation is quite as dear to me—I have labored as honorably for it—as theirs to Washington Irving and Charles Dickens, in whose advocacy this miserable and malignant busybody flounders so laboriously and ostentatiously before the world. I mistake my countrymen greatly if they have it not in their power to teach this person better principles and better manners.

New-York, Nov. 26, 1849 Cornelius Mathews

---

45. *28 November 1849: "Reply to Mr. Mathews"*

Lewis Gaylord Clark in the New York Tribune

Clark asserts in this letter that "Against Mr. Mathews' personal character, aside from his literary pretensions, I have never said nor insinuated a single syllable," a denial he continued to make in two full pages in his Knickerbocker *(Document 48). Nevertheless, in his pertinacious persecution of Mathews, he had written in his* Knickerbocker *(Nov. 1845) that one cannot help thinking that Mathews "has 'a screw loose' somewhere in his mental machinery." That remark caused Poe publicly to call the* Knickerbocker *"beneath notice and beneath contempt." It also provoked Duyckinck to publish a circular letter declaring that the* Knickerbocker *"should be put into Coventry." And William Gilmore Simms was so enraged by Clark's remark that he said in various letters: Clark "is a creature to be kicked or spit upon not argued with or spoken to," and that, "Had I been living in N.Y. I could not have refrained, long ago, to have scourged him hip & thigh for the scoundrel & puppy that he is" (Moss, 86, 103, 104).*

Knickerbocker Sanctum, Tuesday morning, Nov. 27. '49.

To the Editors of The Tribune:

Gentlemen: I am afraid that Mr. Cornelius Mathews was angry when he wrote his card '*To the Press and the Public*,' which appears in this morning's *Tribune*. Those 'be parlous words' wherein he alludes to 'the undersigned,' and yet they are *but* 'words, words,' after all. He complains that I endeavored, in the brief note with which I accompanied the extract from Mr. Dickens's letter which you published, (under a heading of your own prefixing, by the by,) to connect *him* with the 'charges of an infamous nature' which said extract contained against another person. Of the truth of this assertion the readers of that accompanying note can easily judge. Its only reference to Mr. Mathews is a mere allusion to the value of the *comparative criticism* of the writer of 'The Living Authors of England,' as exemplified in his abuse of Washington Irving, and his preference for the 'literary style' and 'philosophical mind' of the author of 'Puffer Hopkins' over those of the author of 'David Copperfield,' 'Oliver Twist,' etc. Not another intimation of any sort can be extorted, or hardly distorted, from the brief note in question.

Against Mr. Mathews' personal character, aside from his literary pretensions, I have never said nor insinuated a single syllable. No; 'the head and front of my offending' is that in common with the 'North American Review,' and other journals of the first critical ability in this country, I have contended, and, with them, do still contend that as a writer Mr. Mathews presents, in the way of literary merit and reputation, a 'product of *nil*.' I have always illustrated and confirmed my own impressions concerning him by quotations from the very best literary minds in America. "Hinc illae lacrimae" [Hence those tears].

The *Evening Mirror*, in a recent and more condemnatory article of Mr. Mathews than I ever penned, speaking of 'the ingenuity which he has long displayed in getting himself puffed,' remarks:

'We question if any native, bold as we are, possesses the hardihood any longer to insist upon his literary merits. Every device that desperate ingenuity could invent has been put into execution and still the public laugh at instead of listening to him. They curl their lips in obdurate scorn and *pish*! at his pretentious importunity.'

Now, gentlemen, ask the *publishers* of the sleepy and sleeping works of the author of 'Puffer Hopkins,'

'Whether or no,
These things be so.'

Good morning, gentlemen:

Yours Faithfully,/L. Gaylord Clark

---

46. *30 November 1849: A Letter to James Gordon Bennett*

Lewis Gaylord Clark in the New York Herald

Clark sends his "Reply to Mathews" (Document 45) to Bennett with a brief introduction.

Knickerbocker Sanctum, Nov. 28, 1849.

Jas. Gordon Bennett, Esq.:

Dear Sir—Will you do me the kindness to insert the enclosed brief rejoinder to the mild and temperate card "To the Press and the Public," by Mr. Cornelius Mathews, author of "Puffer Hopkins and Things?"

Your obed't serv't, L. Gaylord Clark

[Here follows Clark's "Reply to Mr. Mathews."]

---

47. *3 December 1849: A Letter Published in the* Evening Post

Lewis Gaylord Clark

Clark also sends his "Reply to Mathews" (Document 45) to the Evening Post, *again with a brief introduction.*

To the Editors of the Evening Post:

Gentlemen:—Will you oblige me by inserting in the columns of your journal the enclosed response from "*The Tribune*" to the pleasant and quite readable card of the illustrious author of "Puffer Hopkins?" Failing in every thing else, that vast genius seems anxious to be regarded in the light of a *martyr;* but this last resort cannot avail him.

Respectfully yours, L. G. C.

[Here follows Clark's "Reply to Mr. Mathews."]

---

48. *February 1851: Remarks on Cornelius Mathews in the "Editor's Table" of the* Knickerbocker Magazine

Lewis Gaylord Clark

This document, taken out of chronological order, shows how Clark continued to make Mathews ("Puffer Hopkins") a laughingstock. In the process Clark made the unbelievable allegation that Thomas Powell had confessed that Mathews, for Living Authors of England, *had written his own evaluation, one in which he ranked himself above Dickens and even accused Dickens of plagiarizing from him. Clearly, Powell would have been out of his mind to have entrusted such information, so compromisng to himself and Mathews, to anyne, let alone to Clark, the object of his criminal libel suit.*

. . . If it be 'slander' to think and to say that 'Puffer Hopkins' is a literary pretender, ridiculously pertinacious in thrusting his unfounded assumptions of genius and talent before the public, then are we afraid that 'slanders' are very numerous indeed 'in this community.' The many who cry 'Pish!' at the very mention of his name in connection with literature, are 'slanderers'; the dignified and venerable '*North-American Review*,' which has so greatly exceeded the Knickerbocker in the scorching severity of its rebukes of Mr. Hopkins' preposterous literary pretensions, is a 'slanderer'; as are also numerous journals of similar high character, and equally honest and puff-proof, in New-York and elsewhere. . . . Even to mention, on the authority of the writer [Powell] of a work on living American authors, that 'Puffer Hopkins' wrote in that volume [*Living Authors of England*] the description of *himself*, which places him before Dickens, and even accuses the latter of plagiarizing from him!—even this might be considered 'slander!'

---

49. *1 December 1849: Thomas Powell Obtains a Warrant for Hiram Fuller's Arrest*

New York Superior Court

As Powell had threatened, he filed a civil suit for libel against Hiram Fuller, editor/publisher of the New York Mirror, *for publishing "A Scoundrel Branded" (Document 32). Document 61 contains Fuller's "Answer" and "Amended Answer" to Powell's complaint.*

The warrant is a printed form which a clerk fills out and the complainant signs. The printed matter is denoted by square brackets.

In the Superior Court
of the city of New York
Thomas Powell (Plaintiff)
[*against*] [*Undertaking on obtaining order of arrest.*]
Hiram Fuller

[WHEREAS the *plaintiff* in the above entitled action, has made application to] the Superior Court of the city of New York [for an order to arrest the *defendant* therein, do hereby undertake that if the *defendant* recover judgment in the action, the *plaintiff* will pay all costs that may be awarded to the *defendant* and all damages which *he* may sustain by reason of the arrest, not exceeding the sum of] one hundred dollars.

[Dated] December 1st [18]49 [Signed] Thomas Powell
City & County of New York. Thomas Powell, plaintiff above named being duly sworn.

---

50. *7 December 1849: "More Literary Quarrels"*

James Gordon Bennett in the New York Herald

Bennett comments on two "suits of law," one involving Thomas Powell and Lewis Gaylord Clark.

More Literary Quarrels.—Some time ago all the talk was about the amusing quarrel between Gaylord Clark and Charles Dickens, on the one side, and one Powell and Cornelius Mathews on the other. Several shots were fired between the two camps, and some noise created, which rather amused the boys. No harm, it seems, was done.

Another quarrel has been under way at the same time, somewhat connected with this one—a terrible émeute [riot] between Hiram Fuller and George Gordon Byron, the one calling himself a major or a colonel in some military service [as naval storekeeper], and the other a colonel or a major among the invincibles [the British]. Major Byron announced the publication of some unedited letters of his putative father, Lord Byron, and advertised those letters in the newspapers. Major Fuller came down full tilt, in a most savage criticism on those productions, denouncing them as impostures and humbugs. The affair has been going on for some time in the newspapers, by private correspondence, and in suits at law; but both parties seem to be exactly in the same predicament—that is, the game is a drawn one.

---

51. *16 January 1851: Letter to the Editor of the* New York Tribune

"Brief"

Unconscionable trial delays in the city of New York had become notorious. The Herald *(4 Dec. 1849) spoke for many of the metropolitan newspapers in saying that "Great complaints are made respecting the delays occasioned to suitors in our law courts." Even lawyers began to complain, as in this document taken somewhat out of chronological order.*

This situation, of course, proved fortunate for all the parties whom Powell was threatening with libel suits.

"A plea of demurrer," now obsolete in most States, is a plea for the dismissal of a lawsuit on the grounds that even if the statements of the opposition are true, they are insufficient or otherwise legally defective.

To the Editor of the Tribune

The delays in our Courts of Justice are beyond endurance and call for immediate action on the part of our Legislature. Cases which were ready for trial *four* years ago, are now waiting their turn, with no prospect of being reached for a long time to come. A defendant, by interposing a plea of demurrer, can prevent a decision being had for several years, by which time he may be insolvent, or have transferred all his property beyond reach of his creditors.

"Brief"

---

52. *14 December 1849: "Proof (Private and Confidential)"*

Collected by Charles Dickens

Having been alerted by an advertisement (unfound) that Powell's Living Authors of England *might be republished in Britain, if not by Bentley, then by another enterprising publisher, Dickens began to carry out his threat to forestall such an event. If* Living Authors of England *"be republished here by any one," he had declared, "I shall immediately publish my knowledge of*

Mr. Thomas Powell, which is of a rather startling and quite conclusive character" (Document 43).

A more urgent matter that impelled Dickens to collect documents for proof that his alleged libel of Powell was not a libel at all were the reports that Clark had been arrested (Documents 38-40) and had posted bail to assure his appearance before the Grand Jury. Informed of this turn of events rather belatedly, Dickens on 13 December began to collect such documents in great haste. He wrote to Chapman & Co. to solicit information about Powell's criminal history. That information, together with letters signed by John Allan, the junior partner in the Chapman firm, and J. G. Body of New York, as well as a letter from Dr. Southwood Smith about Powell's insanity, was furnished him that very day. Chapman & Co. now had no reluctance to comply with Dickens's request, for even as far away as New York, Powell had continued to defraud the House (see the exchange of letters between J. G. Body and John Allan below) and there was no reason to assume he would not persist in his fraudulent behavior.

These documents, together with The Times article (Document 19), Dickens quickly assembled and sent to Bradbury & Evans, his publishers, whose print shop produced them as a four-page uncut quarto and delivered twenty-five copies to him that very day. There was need for such haste, as Dickens knew that the last steamer to New York was to leave the next day (Document 59).

This copy of the Proof, together with Dickens's covering letter, is at the British Library. An original of the Proof without the covering letter is at the Free Library of Philadelphia.

As only one page of this "rarest item of Dickensiana" has been published (Partington, 19, 20), a facsimile of the full document appears as an Appendix.

There are unexplained differences between this document and the New York Herald report (Document 23) regarding the amount of money and the individuals involved, though the names of John Allan and Richard Bell appear in both accounts. Also, strangely, no entry for J. G. Body appears in the New York City Directory for either 1848-49 or 1849-50.

(PROOF.)

[PRIVATE AND CONFIDENTIAL.]

COPY OF A LETTER FROM MR. CHARLES DICKENS TO MESSRS. JOHN CHAPMAN AND CO., MERCHANTS, 2, LEADENHALL STREET, LONDON.

Devonshire Terrace,
Thursday, 13*th* *December*, 1849.

Dear Sirs,

I beg to call your attention to the accompanying extract, cut from an American newspaper called the "New York Tribune," in which, in a letter to Mr. Clark of New York, I describe Mr. Thomas Powell as "a Forger and a Thief;" and I entreat the favour of your informing me whether he was employed in your house many years, and whether you detected him, at last, in any proceedings which justify that description.

I also beg you to state to me, if you can, when certain criminal charges were preferred against him before the Magistrates at Croydon.

Dear Sir,/Faithfully yours,

Messrs. John Chapman & Co. (Signed) CHARLES DICKENS.

COPY OF A LETTER FROM MESSRS. JOHN CHAPMAN AND CO., MERCHANTS, IN REPLY TO THE FOREGOING.

London, 2, Leadenhall Street,
December 13*th*, 1849.

Sir,

In reply to your letter of this date, inquiring whether the description you gave of our late Clerk, Mr. Thomas Powell, in the American newspaper called the "New York Tribune," wherein you describe him as a "forger and a thief," be correct:—

We beg to inform you that it is too painfully true, we having detected him in a series of frauds, effected both by forgery and peculation, to a large amount.

His examination before the Croydon Magistrates referred to acts committed by him subsequently to his being dismissed from our employment.

We are, Sir,/Your obedient Servants,

Charles Dickens, Esq. (Signed) John Chapman & Co.

[Page] 2

COPY OF A LETTER FROM
DR. SOUTHWOOD SMITH TO
MR. CHARLES DICKENS.

London, *Dec.* 13, 1849.

My Dear Sir,

With reference to a Certificate which I wrote, sometime towards the close of last year, respecting the case of Mr. Thomas Powell, the fact is this: I understood that serious charges were preferred against him before the Magistrates at Croydon; but I most sincerely regarded him as a subject more fit for the lunatic asylum than the prison. I wrote a certificate to that effect, and in consequence of that certificate the charges were not persisted in, but he was taken to a lunatic asylum.

Very truly yours,

Charles Dickens, Esq. (Signed) T. SOUTHWOOD SMITH.

Extract from "The Times," 10th January, 1849.

EXTRAORDINARY CASE.

[This *Times* report is reproduced as Document 19.]

[Page] 3

COPY OF A LETTER from MR. JOHN ALLAN, Partner in the Firm of MESSRS. JOHN CHAPMAN AND CO., to MR. J. G. BODY, of New York, in Answer to a Letter of Advice from that Gentleman, concerning MR. THOMAS

POWELL, who (as will presently appear) by means of fraudulent statements, and the use of a forged Letter of Credit on MESSRS. GEORGE VEASEY AND CO., of Quebec, in MR. ALLAN'S name, had obtained Money from MR. BODY.

London, 30*th August*, 1849.

Dear Sir,

I hasten with feelings of utter astonishment and indignation (as well as sincere regret for your sake) to acknowledge your favour of 14th inst.

Mr. Powell was formerly a clerk in my firm of John Chapman and Co., but left three years ago, having been discovered in acts of fraud and dishonesty, by which he robbed us of a large sum of money. Insanity was pleaded as his excuse, and for the sake of his family we did not prosecute him; afterwards however he was brought before the magistrates for defrauding several tradesmen; again insanity was pleaded, and he was confined for a short time in a lunatic asylum. At length he was sent out of the country by his friends, as the only hope of retrieving his character. This it appears has failed, for I find he has drawn on other parties in London, besides myself, whom, like you, he has most cruelly and wickedly deceived.

By this time he has, no doubt, left New York. I can only therefore deeply regret, that he has succeeded in practising his wicked machinations upon you. I need scarcely add, after what I have said, that every one of his representations are as false, as they are wicked.

I remain, &c.

Mr. J. G. Body. (Signed) JOHN ALLAN.

EXTRACTS FROM A LETTER IN REPLY FROM
MR. J. G. BODY TO
MR. JOHN ALLAN.

New York, 11*th September*, 1849.

Dear Sir,

Deceived by the representations of T. Powell, formerly in your employ, who supported his schemes by producing a Letter of Introduction from you to Messrs. George Veasey, and Co. in Quebec, (copy enclosed,) and also a credit upon the same firm for 250*l.*, I was induced to address a letter to you [ellipses in letter]. I beg you to accept this apology for having addressed you on the subject. A much more cautious man might have been deceived by such a man as Powell, if he would be guilty of forgery [ellipses in letter]. I shall be glad if you will state, for form's sake, if the letter to Messrs. George Veasey and Co., of Quebec, is, or is not, a forgery. Mr. Bell has had Powell before the police, but we have no evidence of the forgery of your name, and he was discharged.

Very respectfully,/Your obedient servant,

John Allan, Esq. (Signed) J. G. BODY.

[Page] 4

COPY OF A LETTER IN REPLY FROM
MR. JOHN ALLAN TO
MR. J. G. BODY OF NEW YORK.

London, 2, Leadenhall Street,
28*th September*, 1849.

Dear Sir,

Referring to my respects to you of the 30th ultimo, I have now to acknowledge your letter of 11th instant, which calls for a renewal of my regret on your behalf, and my astonishment (even after his former delinquencies) of Powell's daring and atrocious proceedings.

I need not add that the assumed letter of introduction to Messrs. George Veasey & Co., is a complete fabrication and forgery, of which I annex formally (in case you should require it) my declaration.

I am, dear Sir,/Very respectfully,

Mr. J. G. Body. (Signed) JOHN ALLAN.

COPY OF THE FORMAL DECLARATION REFERRED TO.

London, 28*th September*, 1849.

Sir,

In reply to your letter of the 11th instant, in which you hand me the following copy of a letter purporting to be signed by me, I beg to acquaint you that the same is a base forgery.

I am, &c.,

Mr. J. G. Body. (Signed) JOHN ALLAN.

COPY OF MR. THOMAS POWELL'S FORGERY, ABOVE DESCRIBED.

London, 2, Leadenhall Street,
April 18*th*, 1849.

Messrs. George Veasey & Co., Quebec.

Dear Sirs,

I beg to introduce to you Mr. Powell, who is about visiting your city. His drafts upon me, to the extent of £250, will meet due honour.

He is authorised by me to enter into negotiation with your firm respecting the establishment of my son. Referring you to him on this matter, and recommending Mr. Powell to your civility,

I am, dear Sir,/Yours very truly,/JOHN ALLAN.

Bradbury and Evans, Printers, Whitefriar

---

53. *14 December 1849: From a Letter to Thomas Chapman*

Charles Dickens

On the same day that Dickens received printed copies of his Proof *(Document 52), he sent one to Chapman with a covering letter.*

My Dear Sir

I am much obliged to you for the enclosed, which has interested and pleased me. I have dispatched matter, by the steamer, enough (in any country but America) to beat this unutterable scoundrel into dust.

Always Faithfully Yours/Charles Dickens

---

54. *14 December 1849: From a Letter to Samuel Phelps*

Charles Dickens

Phelps was a well-known English actor who in all likelihood had read Dickens's exposure of Powell in Clark's letter (Document 32), a letter which had gone the American newspaper rounds and was now going the British rounds too (Documents 56-58).

An "expensive action for Libel" in the letter below refers to Powell's criminal lawsuit against Clark, which, whatever the outcome, would entail legal fees, as well as, if Clark was found guilty, court costs and a possible fine. (In a criminal action, the fine imposed upon a defendant is awarded to the State, not the plaintiff. In addition, the defendant may also suffer the imposition of a prison term.)

Dickens, of course, recognized that he was responsible in great part for Clark's legal predicament, inasmuch as he had written the "libel" of Powell that Clark had had the hardihood to disseminate in "A Scoundrel Branded" (Document 32). Dickens, therefore, was prepared to pay those costs, if his Proof (Document 52) should fail to exculpate Clark.

My Dear Sir

I am much obliged to you for your manly and plain letter in reference to one of the most audacious scoundrels in the world. I send you, in return, a little light I devoted yesterday to the letting in of, upon him. You will see that it is at present *Private and Confidential*. I may have to use it in an expensive action for Libel brought by this immaculate gentleman; and in that case it is very desirable it should be quite fresh and new.

Very Faithfully Yours/[Charles Dickens]

---

55. *14 December 1849: From a Letter to the Editor of the London* Sun

Charles Dickens

Dickens sends Charles Kent, the editor of the London Sun, *a copy of his* Proof *(Document 52). Neither Kent nor any other newspaper editor in England (P, 5:672n) or America published any portion of the* Proof.

Private and Confidential.

Sir.

I depart from the usual course in addressing you thus, and in forwarding to you a Proof I have had privately printed for this purpose only, under special circumstances.

Being advised from America that "Mr. Thomas Powell, a literary gentleman from England," was about to enter on a course of scurrility and libel there, which he had already begun by publishing a "Life" of myself, in all respects utterly false; and knowing Mr. Powell's history and the certainty of his proceeding in this course to any extent, unless summarily stopped; I deemed it necessary to expose him. I therefore wrote to a friend [Clark] in New York that the Mr. Powell in question was "a Forger and a Thief", and had been confined as a Lunatic besides—and requested him to publish that piece of intelligence.

It appeared, I learn from my friend, in a great many American Newspapers, being copied from one into another; and the Mail which arrived yesterday informs me that there is now much virtuous discussion and threatening of actions for libel, among them, on the subject. *With no view whatever to the publication of the facts in this country* (which, indeed, I wish to avoid if possible) but simply that, in case any of these numerous references to the matter should meet your eye, you should be possessed of the facts, I take the liberty as between two gentlemen to forward them to you, as I have collected them within a few hours.

I am Sir/Your faithful Servant/Charles Dickens

56. *22 December 1849: "Anglo-American and Journalist Row"*

William Jerdan in the London Literary Gazette

News of the quarrel between Dickens and Powell, which was embroiling New York newspapers in controversy, crosses the ocean, as is evident in this summary of the vendetta.

William Jerdan was owner and editor of the long-lived and very successful Literary Gazette.

The remarks on Dickens's alleged railway speculations appear in the Headnote to Document 41.

When our brethren across the Atlantic quarrel, they do it in earnest, and carry the flowers of vituperation to the highest (or, *quaere*, lowest) pitch of which the English language, refined in America, is capable. The present outbreak, as we gather from the *New York Herald* of the 26th ult., has originated in the publication of a life of Mr. Dickens by a Mr. Thomas Powell. The work in which this appeared is published by Messrs. Appletons, and entitled "The Living Authors of England;" and Mr. Dickens, aggrieved by its contents, writes a letter to Mr. L. Gaylord Clark on the subject, denouncing Mr. Powell's biography as "from beginning to end one intact and complete lie." Mr. Powell is, nevertheless, said to be puffed in the *New York Evening Post*; and Mr. Clark, as a counterpoise, and under the heading, in capitals, of "A SCOUNDREL BRANDED," has a letter inserted in the *New York Tribune* newspaper (which, as well as the *Mirror*, had copied some of Powell's, or the *Post*'s statements), with an extract from Mr. Dickens' communication to him, as an enclosure. Of this, besides the strong passage already quoted, the following is the concluding portion:—

"I think Mr. Powell a very likely man, indeed, to form a ready connexion with the American press. He is a forger and a thief." [The rest of Dickens's letter appears in Document 28.]

In the *New York Herald*, already referred to, these particulars are given at length, with a sort of running commentary and rejoinder; charging Mr. Dickens with having been infected with the railroad mania through the agency of Powell, and spattering everybody named with a pretty equal distribution of dirt. [The remainder of this quotation concerning railroad speculation appears in Document 41.]

Ex gr[atia].:—

"With the railway explosion, all hands were diddled, Powell's employers were tricked, Dickens was cheated, and Powell was ruined—the railroad king and his satellites, the speculators and the subscribers, fell together in the crash, like Nicholas Biddle, Watson Webb, the banks, and their victims, in 1837. Powell escaped to this country, and for a livelihood commenced writing the book entitled "The Living Authors of England," of which the Appletons are the publishers. The sketches are small gossip, which don't amount to much; but they appear to have hit the sensitive feelings of Dickens, who, since his brilliant reception by our codfish aristocracy, and the honours of the 'Boz ball,' has become exceedingly consequential and exclusive. He writes to Mr. Clark (a literary man, with a good deal of extra superfine common sense), his complaints and charges against Mr. Powell. Mr. Clark, of course, could not keep a letter from Dickens from the knowledge of the world, and so he forthwith publishes it with a flourish of trumpets and kettle-drums, in the *Tribune*. The *Mirror*, and some other papers, with as little remorse or delicacy, take up the echo of 'a scoundrel branded,' and republish the correspondence without qualification or apology. Powell was thunderstruck, cut up, knocked down, trampled upon. No one could suppose that philosopher Greeley would brand "a man a scoundrel' unless the fact were so. But Powell soon recovered from the shock; and now comes the reaction.

"Civil and criminal suits are to be instituted against the offending parties—Gaylord Clark, Horace Greeley, Hiram Fuller, the Naval Storekeeper, and all others concerned in the publication with a malicious intent. The trial will require the proofs, the facts, the tangible legal evidence, to support the accusations of Mr. Dickens. His mere unsupported declarations will simply amount to a libel. What then follows, if Powell convicts these parties of this offence? We tremble to mention it. The philosopher Greeley, the financier McElrath, Mr. Clark, the literary man—the American Dickens—and Hiram Fuller, the Naval Storekeeper, may all possibly become the boon companions of Ned Buntline before the next summer is over. The muses, the Fourierites, and the Naval Storekeeper, will have to go to Blackwell's Island, and probably work in the shoe shop at that place. What a galaxy of stars will be there! We shall look with most intense anxiety to the conclusion of this affair. Meantime, let the ten governors make all needful preparations for the proper reception of these distinguished guests on Blackwell's Island, if need be. Everybody will now want to read Powell's book. Appletons are the publishers. Go and buy it."

As with the Postscript to a Lady's letter, the whole gist of this diatribe lies in the concluding two lines, and the advice, "Go and buy Powell's book!" To make the gruel more "thick and slab," we have only to add, that a Mr. Cornelius Mathews had entered the lists, and calls Mr. Gaylord Clark, in regard to himself, "a malignant and persevering libeller," and protests against his writings as dastardly, wholly unprovoked, and most impudent contrivances of insatiable malice.

For ourselves, we must believe that Mr. Dickens would not have sketched the life of Powell as he has done, without being well able to sustain the responsibility of such grave accusations; but how his proofs may be made available for defence against Powell's suits in the law courts of America, we are not lawyers enough to determine.

---

57. *25 December 1849: Response to the Editor of the* Literary Gazette

Charles Dickens

The laureate of Christmas caps the holiday by sending the editor of the Literary Gazette *a copy of* Proof *(Document 52) for his private perusal.*

My Dear [William] Jerdan

Merry Christmas and happy new Year!

As you reprint the extraordinary lies of the New York Herald, perhaps you may like to know something more of their authority. I therefore send you for your own perusal (for I must not anticipate the defence to the ingenious Mr. Powell's American actions for libel) a few small passages in the life of the distinguished "literary gentleman from England," who is in question.

Faithfully Yours always/CD

---

58. *22 December 1849:* The Manchester Examiner and Times *on Thomas Powell*

Dispatched by Its London Correspondent

Only one issue of The Manchester Examiner *of this date exists in the entire world—at the British Library's Newspaper Library. Not even the Manchester Central Library has this issue, a situation made odder by the fact that the editor of* The Manchester Examiner*—Alexander Ireland—had been a founding member of the Library in 1851.*

The London Correspondent discusses Powell's Living Authors of England *("would disgrace a costermonger"), his connection with "all the eminent literary men of the day," the discovery of his defalcations and his consequent attempt at suicide and internment for madness, and how his literary friends and employers united to save him from transportation by sending him to America.*

Your readers have read in your columns of one Mr. Thomas Powell, and his paltry book on English Authors. His history is sufficiently instructive. Some four or five years back he lived, I think, at Peckham. At all events, he had a house somewhere in the vicinity of that suburb, and was known for his profuse hospitality, his greed for popularity, and his anxiety to make a distinguished literary connection. He gave sumptuous banquets, and all the eminent literary men of the day—Leigh Hunt and Dickens amongst them—were his guests. He published light papers, and some volumes of plays—was profuse in his expenditure, large in his bounties, and was engaged in some capacity in the firm of Messrs. Chapman Brothers, of the City. It was, at last, suspected that all was not right; and, on examination, it appeared that he had come dishonestly by the funds which he had so liberally dispensed. On the eve of this discovery, it is said that he attempted suicide. His literary friends, in the most charitable spirit, gathered round him, as did his employers; and by the united kindness of these gentlemen he was saved, probably from transportation. It was reported that he was mad; and after a temporary retirement, he embarked for America; where, it is reported, he has forged upon London houses more than once. Such a history would, most people would think, sober a man's love of popularity—not so that of Mr.

Thomas Powell. He has turned upon those who shielded him in his disgrace, and published a book that would disgrace a costermonger. I have certainly not seen the performance, but I have heard a very ample description of it; and for vituperation and shamelessness it is allowed to be, on all hands, a masterpiece.

---

59. *24 December 1849: From a Letter to the Editor of* The Manchester Examiner and Times

Charles Dickens

Dickens asks Alexander Ireland, the editor of The Manchester Examiner, *to print a retraction of the statement that he had ever feasted in Powell's house, a request that Ireland did not satisfy (P, 5:678n). (Dickens failed to add that Powell had feasted at his house.) The novelist, moreover, enclosed a copy of his* Proof *(Document 52) to indicate why he did not wish to be associated with such a person.*

Emerson (15, 189) said that The Manchester Examiner *was a "powerful local journal," and that Ireland (who had arranged to underwrite Emerson's fees for his 1847-48 British lecture tour) was a "man of sense and of letters [who] added to his solid virtues an infinite sweetness and* bonhomie.*"*

My Dear Sir

You will not be offended by my saying that (in common with many other men) I think "our London correspondent" one of the great nuisances of this time, in as much as our London Correspondent, seldom knowing anything, feels bound to know everything, and becomes in consequence a very reckless gentleman in respect of the truthfulness of his intelligence.

In your paper sent to me this morning, I see the Correspondent mentions one Thomas Powell, and records how I was wont to feast in the house of the said Thomas Powell. As I never was in the man's house in my life, or within five miles of it that I know of, I beg you will do me the favor to contradict this.

You will be the less surprised by my begging you to set this right, when I tell you that hearing of his book, and knowing his history, I wrote to New York denouncing him as "a Forger and a

Thief." That he thereupon put the gentleman who published my letter into Prison. And that having but one day before the sailing of the last steamer to collect the proofs printed in the accompanying sheet (which are but a small part of the Villain's life) I got them together in that time, and sent them out, to justify the character I gave him. It is not agreeable to me, to be supposed to have sat at this amiable person's feasts.

Faithfully Yours/Charles Dickens

---

60. *29 December 1849: From a Letter to the Editor of* **The Manchester Examiner and Times**

Charles Dickens

Alexander Ireland, as editor of The Manchester Examiner, *asked Dickens's permission to publish the* Proof *that the novelist had sent him, since it was marked PRIVATE AND CONFIDENTIAL.*

My Dear Sir

I am much obliged to you for your note. I do *not* wish the papers to be published at present (and therefore have prevented their appearance here), because I wish to explode them on this most consummate Villain, in America.

Faithfully Yours/Charles Dickens

---

61. *2 & 18 January 1850: Hiram Fuller's Answer and Amended Answer to Thomas Powell's Complaint of Libel*

New York Superior Court

In response to a request concerning Powell's rumored libel suits against Horace Greeley, Hiram Fuller, and Charles Dickens, the present County Clerk and Clerk of the Supreme Court of New York (who is also in charge of the Division of Old Records), states: "These [including Document 49] are the only documents that have survived."

In the Superior Court
Of the city of New York
Thomas Powell (Plaintiff)
——against—— Answer
Hiram Fuller (Defendant)
City and County of New York

The defendant for answer to the complaint of the plaintiff states:

1st. That he admits he is the publisher of a newspaper as charged in the complaint.

2nd. He admits the publication of the article as charged in the complaint, but he insists that it was copied as an item of news from the New York Tribune, a newspaper published in the city of New York, and that he is informed and believes that no suit has been instituted by the plaintiff for the recovery of damages against the publishers of that paper for the publication thereof.

3rd. The defendant further states that he copied said article as an item of news without any malice against the said plaintiff and because he believed the matters stated therein to be true, judging from the source from whence they emanated and the character of the paper in the columns of which the article appeared.

4th. The defendant denies that the plaintiff, by reason of the publication of said article, has been injured or damnified to any amount whatever.

5th. The defendant states that he has been informed, and believes such to be the fact, that previous to the publication of said article by the defendant, the plaintiff had been arrested and imprisoned for obtaining money upon a letter of credit purporting to have been drawn by John Allan of the well known firm of Chapman & Co. of London, the name of the said John Allan having been forged by the said plaintiff, and that fact was published in the columns of the Mirror, as well as by other newspapers in the city of New York, as an item of police intelligence *before* the publication of the article which the plaintiff has made the foundation for this suit.

6th. The defendant insists that, according to the best of his information and belief, the matters contained in said article which are made the ground for this action against the defendant are true; and as one of the reasons for entertaining this belief is the fact that a criminal charge for obtaining money upon a letter

of credit forged by him has been made against the plaintiff before one of the magistrates in this city, and he has been arrested to answer said charge before the proper tribunal, which charge against the said plaintiff has not yet been brought to trial.
[Signed] Hiram Fuller

Bedinger & Chase, Defendant Attorneys, City and County of New York

[R. C. Morrant, Jr., Plaintiff Attorney, City and County of New York]

Hiram Fuller, the defendant above named being duly sworn, says that he has read the above answer subscribed by him, and that the same is true of his own knowledge except about the matters which are therein stated to be on his information and belief, and as to those matters he believes them to be true.

Sworn to before me
the 2nd day of Jany 1850 [Signed] Hiram Fuller
[Signed] M. S. Brewster
Commissioner of Records

N. Y. Superior Court
Thomas Powell)
ag[ain]st) Allegations in Defendant's answer numbered
Hiram Fuller) "5" as amended in obedience to order of Court

The defendant states that he has been informed & believes that previous to the publication of the said article, the plaintiff had been arrested & imprisoned for obtaining money upon a letter of credit purporting to have been drawn by John Allan of the well known firm of Chapman & Co. of London; to which letter of credit the plaintiff had forged the name of the said John Allan, and he states further that the fact of the plaintiff's having been thus arrested & imprisoned was published in the columns of the Evening Mirror as well as in other newspapers in the city of New York, as an item of police intelligence before the publication of the article which the plaintiff has made the foundation of this suit.

Dated 18th Jany 1850 [Signature illegible]
Beringer & Chase
Defendant's attys.
City and County of New York

Hiram Fuller the Defendant above named being duly sworn says that he has read the above allegations (as amended) subscribed by him, and that the same are true of his own knowledge except as to the matters which are therein stated to be on his information or belief and as to those matters he believes them to be true.

Sworn before me the [Signature illegible]
18th day of Jany 1850
[Signed] M. S. Brewster
Court of Records

---

62. *25 January 1850: Thomas Powell Sues Dickens for Libel*

Charles Dickens

James Gordon Bennett had reported that, on Powell's complaint, a magistrate had issued a warrant for the arrest of Clark to answer to the charge of libel (Document 38)—a complaint confirmed by the New York Police Court Docket Book and by the Tribune *(Document 40). However, apart from these confirmations, the evidence of any further proceedings in the case is entirely negative. The case does not appear in the Minutes of the New York Court of General Sessions or in the General Sessions Indictment Papers. Also, there never appeared in the* Knickerbocker *any allusion to Powell's charge against Clark, nor was there any suspension in the publication of the magazine or of the "Editor's Table." Neither do any of Clark's extant letters (Dunlap) refer prospectively or retrospectively to Powell or to prison or trial. Moreover, though many New York newspapers ran columns devoted to "Police Intelligence," "Legal Intelligence," and "Court Cases," no reference was found to Clark being tried or, for that matter, Greeley and Fuller, editors who had published Clark's letter (Document 32). Nor is Clark, Fuller, or Greeley cited in "The Table of Cases" published in the* Decennial Edition of the American Digest, *which constitutes a complete digest of all* reported *American legal cases from 1658 to 1906. Thus the conclusion is irresistible, especially given the fragments in "Thomas Powell against Hiram Fuller" (Documents 49 & 61), that Powell's complaints of libel against Clark, Fuller, and Greeley were quashed, indicative that a ruling came down that, as* *none of these individuals were the originators of the alleged libel, but the mere transmitters of it, the only culpable libeler was Charles Dickens himself. Hence the civil suit that Powell brought against Dickens for $10,000.*

Augustus, now twenty-three, was Dickens's youngest brother and still an accountant in the House of Chapman & Co.

John Barrow, Dickens's cousin who was living in New York, was the person who put Dickens in touch with "one of the first Lawyers in New York," though the lawyer's identity is unknown. That lawyer was now urging Dickens to secure "office copies of the depositions taken . . . in the case of Thomas Powell" to be used as evidence in court (Document 63).

Though the lawsuit would have been the stuff of juicy gossip, no reference to it was found in the letters of such British and American contemporaries as Richard Monckton Milnes, Mary Russell Mitford, Thackeray, Trollope, the Carlyles, the Longfellows, and James Russell Lowell.

My Dear Augustus.

I wish you would shew the enclosed letter to "the House". It is from one of the first Lawyers in New York, and points out what I *must* do, in defending [against] this Scoundrel's action. He lays his damages at 10,000 dollars!

If you will endeavour to get the information provided for me, I will call tomorrow (Saturday) in Leadenhall Street, at from three to half past.

Affecy. Always/CD.

---

63. *8 February 1850: Dickens Requests Copies of Depositions Relevant to Thomas Powell's Libel Suit*

Charles Dickens

Chapman & Co., not wishing to be drawn into a libel suit that threatened to be bruited at home and abroad, did not provide Dickens with copies of the depositions he wanted (Document 62), depositions that their lawyers had taken in their investigation of Powell's embezzlements. Thus, after waiting two weeks, Dickens, perhaps with Augustus's contrivance, wrote to Henry Richards, another Chapman employee, to re-request the deposi-

tions. With or without official consent, Richards provided them, and Dickens had twenty-five of them printed (P, 6:33n), as he had similarly done with the "Proof."

This extract is from a Parke-Bernet Galleries catalog of November 1967 (P, 6:33). The fragmentariness of the letter and the ellipses are those of the catalog writer.

. . . having been informed by my brother that you were so kind as to arrange with him for letting me have office copies of the depositions taken . . . in the case of Thomas Powell . . . it is most important that I should be in possession of them today to send to America.

---

64. *2 February 1850:* The Literary World *Reviews Thomas Powell's* The Living Authors of America: First Series

Evert A. Duyckinck

On 29 January 1850 an advertisement in the Evening Post *announced that Powell's new book would appear in two days and declared: "There has been no literary work of late issued so well calculated to challenge the attention of the American public."*

The book, however, put Duyckinck's teeth on edge, but he reviewed it as good-naturedly as he could in the circumstances.

An odd agglomeration of small talk, "leetle" anecdotes, criticism, elegant extracts, occasional acuteness, and sheer balderdash—literary cockneyism and Joe Miller combined. On the presumption that it is a book of sober criticism, as the title imports, it would be liable to severe animadversion for its looseness of style, and absurd, insolent manner; but taken on the other side, as a money-making squib, it is amusing to witness the shifts and resources with which the writer ekes out his treatment of a dull topic, on his hands, of which he knows little and cares less. Powell's Authors of England professed to be derived from personal knowledge of the writers, and was at least entertaining as a collection of amusing stories drawn from a certain level of English society. The sting was taken from its wanton spirit of mischief by its utter recklessness.

STRINGER & TOWNSEND
HAVE JUST PUBLISHED:

THE LIVING AUTHORS OF AMERICA.
FIRST SERIES.

Containing Critical and Anecdotical Sketches of the following writers: COOPER, EMERSON, WILLIS, POE, LONGFELLOW, PRESCOTT, BRYANT, HALLECK, DANA, OSGOOD, FULLER, KIRKLAND, SPARKS.

Muslin bound. Price $1.00.

PICTURES

OF THE

LIVING AUTHORS

OF

BRITAIN.

BY THOMAS POWELL,

AUTHOR OF "PICTURES OF THE LIVING AUTHORS OF AMERICA."

LONDON:
PARTRIDGE & OAKEY, PATERNOSTER ROW.

MDCCCLI.

Top: Ad in *The Literary World.*
Thomas Powell's name as author is conspicuously absent, probably because of his recent encounter with the police.

Bottom: Title page of the shortened version of *The Living Authors of England.*

[Here Duyckinck added a footnote: "It is but a simple act of justice to Mr. Dickens to state, that in a letter printed extensively in the American newspapers, he has denounced in the most express terms, as utterly false, the anecdotes, &c, published of him in the Living Authors of England."]

The book on the living authors of America has no story to tell, and what little mischief is intended is so puerile in style and idea, that it is simply ridiculous. We can give no better idea of the volume than by calling to mind an inflated fourth rate English provincial actor on a fourth rate American stage gagging furiously, interpolating Cooper and Bryant, serious with a verse of Thanatopsis, comical with a twist of buffoonery; straining his perceptions into the Buccaneer one moment, and his relaxed head through a horse-collar the next.

Running rapidly over the book we have hit upon a hundred such comicalities as these, with now and then a bit of good sense tersely expressed. They are curiosities of literature, Mr. Powell's book being perfectly unique.

[Here Duyckinck gives examples of Powell's "comicalities" such as this: "We have the authority of one of the poet's own family for saying that Queen Victoria . . . had never heard of Wordsworth till he was proposed to her for Poet Laureate."]

We should not spoil so good a story by introducing after it any of Mr. Powell's serious fun in his rhapsodies, reflections, and critiques, so we cut short our extracts while the reader is in a good humor with this, all things considered, most extraordinary piece of literary composition.

---

65. *7 March 1850: From a Letter to a Former Publisher of Thomas Powell*

Charles Dickens

Effingham Wilson had published three works by Powell, The Count de Foix: A Tale of Olden Times, A Poem *(1842);* Poems *(1842); and* The Shepherd's Well, *a play (1843). Having read Dickens's denunciation of Powell as reported in the* Literary Gazette *or* The Manchester Examiner, *Wilson had written to the novelist to provide him with additional revelations about his former friend.*

The strange thing is that, neither in England nor America, was there a word of gossip about Powell's lawsuit against Dickens, one of the most newsworthy people in the world.

Dear Sir

I beg you will accept my very cordial thanks for the letter you have had the goodness to write to me, in reference to the case of Thomas Powell. I have no serious apprehension of the success of that Rascal; but a manful communication like yours is very important assistance towards that entire demolition of him which I hope to effect—only because I know him to be so irreclaimable and dangerous a criminal, that society cannot bear him.

Faithfully Yours/Charles Dickens

---

66. *10 March 1850: From a Letter to Augustus Dickens*

Charles Dickens

Thomas Chapman, wishing to become a member of the Parthenon Club, wanted Dickens to exert his influence on his behalf, and indirectly contacts him through his brother.

Dickens had been a member of the Parthenon, a select dining club, from 1838 to 1845. John Wylie Barrow was a cousin of the Dickenses who secured a lawyer to represent Dickens in Powell's libel suit against him (Headnote to Document 62).

My Dear Augustus.

I should have been quite delighted to do all in my power for Mr. Chapman, but that I have retired from the Parthenon some years—five, I should think.

Pray tell John Barrow that I am much obliged to him for his kind and valuable assistance in the matter of the slandered Powell.

Affecy. always/Charles Dickens

---

67. *1851:* Pictures of the Living Authors of Britain

Thomas Powell

This pocket-sized version of the Living Authors of England *was published in London by Partridge & Oakey, and contained only fifteen of the original thirty-eight essays. Oddly, the title on the title page (given above) differed from that on the spine, which read* Living Authors of England.

Only the final sentence (see below) of the essay on Dickens (Document 22) was omitted.

No review or reaction to this "reprint" has been found.

It was said, at the time, that his [Dickens's] salary [on *The Daily News*] was one hundred pounds per week, an amount equal, we are told, to an *entire year's* pay of many men of talent for editing leading daily papers in New-York.

THE VENDETTA ENDS

"What can't be cured must be endoored"
—Captain Cuttle in *Dombey and Son*

68. *2 May 1852: From a Letter to Lewis Gaylord Clark*

Charles Dickens

Dickens's legal entanglement with Powell had thus far been protracted for two years and three months and, past being prologue, it threatened to continue interminably, like the case of Jarndyce and Jarndyce *in* Bleak House, *whose first installment had appeared in March 1852. Faced with that bleak prospect, Dickens decided to terminate Powell's libel suit against him by settling out of court, for what sum cannot be determined, as Coutts & Co., Dickens's banker, has no record of the transaction.*

A tantalizing bit in a Powell letter to Duyckinck, who was Powell's adviser—"I will do nothing final *without your advice" (Document 36)—may refer to that culmination: ". . . Last letters from England have been very satisfactory & materially change the aspect of affairs." Unfortunately, the letter, as all of Powell's letters to Duyckinck, is undated.*

Apart from the single fact that Dickens settled with Powell, a vacuum exists in regard to evidence. Of various explanations, three seem plausible. One is that the documents (the Proof *and the Depositions) that Dickens sent his New York lawyer lacked authentication and were therefore in the nature of hearsay, inasmuch as those who purportedly signed the documents could not be examined in person. Indeed, in England William Jerden had wondered how Dickens could sustain his "grave accusations" against Powell in American law courts (Document 56). And in America Bennett had predicted that Dickens will require "tangible legal evidence," else his "unsupported declarations will simply amount to a libel" (Document 41).*

The second possibility is that Dickens felt the game was no longer worth the candle, especially as his first-class New York lawyer must have been charging him first-class fees in a case that had no foreseeable conclusion, let alone a guarantee of a successful outcome. By this time Dickens may have learned that it "is the cost of defending, not the risk of paying damages, that unnerves the . . . libel defendant" (Gillmor, 13). For "whatever the precise figure at any particular time and in any particular place, legal fees constitute as much as 80 percent of the aggregate costs of a defense, court costs and damage awards constituting the remainder" (ibid., 20). Thurlow Weed, an American acquaintance of Dickens, had to pay $17,000 in costs in a libel suit he won against James Fenimore Cooper (ibid., 58), which must have put him in mind of Voltaire's rueful remark: "I was ruined twice—once when I lost a case and once when I won a case."

A third possibility is that Dickens was facing the prospect of being declared malicious, something that the newspapers were bound to sensationalize. If the law, as Mr. Bumble says in Oliver Twist, is a ass, a idiot, judges do not always escape that aspersion, for their latitute of interpretation is so great as to seem capricious at times. Indeed, a law book by two law professors opens with the declaration: "The search for certainty in the law is a search for a chimera" (Christie & Phillips). The ruling under which Dickens acted states "That the truth of libelous statements is a complete justification in a civil action, notwithstanding [that] the libel is malicious." But another ruling states "That the truth of libel is not a defence, unless the motive in publishing it is good" (Century Digest, 32:2074). A malicious libeler is, by definition, one who holds up an individual "to ridicule, contempt, shame, disgrace, or obloquy [and] to degrade him in the estimation of the community" (Black, 915). A verdict of malicious libel might well have damaged the novelist's reputation for Christian charity upon which sales of his serials, books, and magazines greatly depended. Thus, Dickens, always concerned about his readers' opinion, probably decided to wash his hands of the entire affair. As he indicates in the letter below, he had had enough of American lawyers and law, which he found to be as bad as England's. He thus became indifferent to the fate of the Proof and Depositions, as they had proved useless; and from this point he all but ceased communication with Clark, who had cooperated with him in getting them into legal messes. One exception to this breach with Clark occurred on 30 December 1852 when Dickens rejected Clark's Knick-Knacks from an Editor's Table for Household Words. Two other exceptions occurred *some fifteen years later when Dickens was in America on his reading tour.*

"To you and yours" refers to the fact that in 1842 on Dickens's first trip to the States, Clark had entertained Dickens and his wife Catherine at his house, where they met Mrs. Clark (née Ella Maria Curtis) and their five children.

"We Are Seven" is the title of a Wordsworth poem, whose child speaker sees death only as an absence and insists that her dead brother and sister are alive.

My Dear Clark

. . . I have received your letter concerning the Powellian Vagabond, and will take care that the money is paid. When I find that I am made to smart to that extent for saving your fellow citizens from a Swindler, I begin to think your law must be as bad as ours—I can't think worse of it. I can't advise you as to the publication of the evidence. You must judge for yourself. I have no wish or care, either way.

We are all well, and Mrs. Dickens unites with me in kind remembrances to you and yours. "We are seven"—and two over. Have been three over, but a real little Dora closely followed her imaginary namesake to the Land of Shadows.

Faithfully Yours always/Charles Dickens

---

69. *13 December 1851 & 31 May 1852: Last Letters to Thomas Chapman*

Charles Dickens

The final letters that Dickens wrote to Thomas Chapman were business-like and rather formal, though his brother Augustus would continue to work for Chapman & Co. until 1855. Clearly, the two men had become estranged. Dickens noted in the second letter below that "it seems so long since we met."

There were minor reasons for the estrangement. Dickens had made himself something of a nuisance in securing documents and depositions from Chapman & Co. He had also announced to at least four members of the press, let alone to an unknown number of private individuals, that the great House of Chapman & Co. had been prey to embezzlement and fraud, an exposure that the House could not have appreciated, especially when all that disturbance and disclosure went for nothing, as matters turned out. But the principal reason for their falling out seems to have been the portrait of Chapman as Dombey. Even granting that Chapman did not see himself in that portrait (which is a stretch indeed), others did, and it could not help offending a man no less sensitive than Dickens and who, if such things can be compared, was as important in commerce, finance, and technology as Dickens was in literature.

If Chapman needed further evidence that, to one degree or another, he had been portrayed as Dombey (Headnote to Document 27), it was being assigned a young daughter—a reflection of Chapman's only child, his daughter Ethel Maria, whom Dickens had met when she was not yet fourteen.

Like Florence Dombey, Miss Chapman eventually married (her husband was Eugene Frederick Noel) and, again like Miss Dombey, she bore two children. Inasmuch as Chapman's wife had died, his daughter was his chief beneficiary (Chapman's Will).

My Dear Sir:

Will you allow me to present to you, Mr. [William Henry] Wills—who is my confidential friend and assistant in the management of Household Words, and on whom I have the fullest reliance—to explain to you a scheme he has originated in connexion with mercantile and shipping matters, and in which he has already much interested some high authorities? I cannot do him a better service, I am sure, than by giving him an occasion of stating his views to you; and I hope you will find them practical, clear, and worthy of attention. Indeed I am sure you will, or I would not trouble you with this note.

My Dear Sir/Faithfully Yours always/Charles Dickens

My Dear Sir

I am precluded from having an article in Household Words on the subject to which the enclosed note refers, because such Institutions have been already especially noticed in that Journal. Many months have elapsed since they were strongly advocated, and their principal features of merit described.

Otherwise I should have been truly happy in this case, as in any other, to respond to a wish of yours.

Mrs. Dickens unites with me in kind regards to Mrs. Chapman. I suppose your Daughter is not married yet? Time flies so fast, and it seems so long since we met, that I have a dim and general impression of her being almost *twenty*!!

My Dear Sir/Very faithfully Yours/Charles Dickens

---

70. *"Heep and Powell: Dickensian Revenge?"*

Stanley Friedman

As the title of this article in The Dickensian *suggests (for melodramatic Victorian novels require that a villain be exposed and excoriated), Dickens's anger toward Powell was intense, and he continued the vendetta in* David Copperfield *(1849-50) in the guise of Uriah Heep (another version of James Carker).*

Heep, with his cadaverous face and close-cropped red hair and his insistence that he is a very umble person, bears no resemblance to Powell. Indeed, Powell was said to be "The Original Micawber"—the title of his obituary in the New York Mirror *(29 Jan. 1887) written by "Nestor" who claimed to be "the first man in America connected with literature whom Powell called on." Powell, he added, "was never known to make any direct reference to Micawber, but was able to produce very strong evidence that he had held most friendly relations with the author in whose book that character figured. . . . If Phiz' pictures are of any authority, they represent such a person as Powell in full fig." Friedman (42n) acknowledges that earlier scholars like Kitton, Pugh, and Wright "suggest that Powell, like Dickens's own father, served as a model for some of the traits displayed by Micawber."*

Late in *David Copperfield* Mr Micawber . . . tells David, Traddles, Aunt Betsey, and Mr Dick of Uriah Heep's criminal behaviour: "Villa[i]ny is the matter; baseness is the matter; deception, fraud, conspiracy, are the matter; and the name of the whole atrocious mass is—HEEP! (Ch. XLIX).

Continuing the tirade, Micawber employs epithets like 'the abandoned rascal', 'interminable cheat, and liar', and 'consummate scoundrel'. . . . Subsequently, in the great comic exposure scene, he confronts and angrily excoriates Uriah: 'a scoundrel', 'probably the most consummate Villain that has ever existed', 'the Forger and the Cheat' (Ch. LII).

---

71. *22 & 29 January 1887: "The Late Thomas Powell" from* **Frank Leslie's Illustrated Newspaper** *and "The Original Micawber" from the* **New York Mirror**

Almost everyone knows about Dickens's life subsequent to the vendetta, but about Powell's very little is known, though his obituaries appeared in major New York newspapers and though he was canonized by inclusion in The Oxford Companion to American Literature *and the* Dictionary of American Biography. *He even received a two-sentence death notice in the London* Times *(15 January 1887) that read: "The death is announced of Mr. Thomas Powell, a well-known writer. The deceased was a native of England."*

Only two of these obituaries are presented here, as they were written by men who knew Powell. Frank Leslie was the Rupert Murdoch of his time, and Powell worked in his newspaper and magazine empire for over thirty years. The other was written by "Nestor" who claimed to be "the first man in America connected with literature whom Powell called on." The New York Mirror, *by the way, was one of the papers that Powell had wanted to sue for disseminating Dickens's libel. The other obituaries, published in the* New York Times *and the* New York Tribune, *were written by strangers and are, by and large, mere bibliographical accounts of Powell's literary and journalistic ventures.*

In no obituary or biographical entry is there any mention of Powell's felonious behavior or his vendetta with Dickens. To all appearances he had lived out his days without further encounters with police or recourse to insane asylums. Indeed, he earned a certain celebrity in journalistic and literary circles and came to be known as "The Original Micawber." A Colonel Rush C. Hawkins, in whose regiment Powell's son Frank served as a sergeant during the Civil War, annotated one of Powell's letters to him with a certain awe: "The writer of this was the original of Micawber—so I have heard" (Brown University Library).

In two Dickens bibliographies, Eckel remarked that "Powell died . . . a suicide." Powell's death certificate, however, signed by H. C. Hendry, M.D., certifies that he died from complications of "chronic cerebral meningitis, chronic tubular nephritis, and hepatic enlargement." (The undertaker added that Powell was to be buried in New York Bay Cemetery.)

John Brougham, cited below as Powell's co-editor of the Lantern, *was an Irish-born playwright/actor who dramatized* Dombey and Son, David Copperfield, *and* Bleak House *for the stage.*

William Stuart, christened Edmund O'Flaherty, had been an MP in Ireland, but, like Powell, he had engaged in fraud and fled to New York City to escape prosecution. A dramatic critic and theatrical manager, he was, again like Powell, a gourmet and entertained many notable people from both continents in the clubs that he frequented.

The Late Thomas Powell

The death of Thomas Powell, at Newark, New Jersey, on Thursday of last week removed from the field of letters and journalism one of its distinguished veterans. His literary activity, which began fifty years ago, continued almost up to the day of his death; and the readers of his "Leaves from my Life," in the last few numbers of *Frank Leslie's Sunday Magazine,* can testify that age did not wither nor custom stale the vivacious charm of his pen. His books have been published and read on both sides of the Atlantic. He was the first editor of *Frank Leslie's Illustrated Newspaper*, the initial number of which appeared December 15th, 1855: he saw his pioneer periodical take and maintain its place at the head of American illustrated journalism, and his connection with the house founded by the late Frank Leslie has been continuous during thirty-two years.

Poet, critic, journalist and wit, and industrious worker withal, Mr. Powell did not belong to the distinctively Bohemian class of the past generation; and yet he was one of its circle of choicest spirits and *bon vivants,* which included such men as Artemus Ward, John Brougham, Tom Picton, Charles Gayler, Frank Ottarson, Will Stuart, and a score of others whose names are equally familiar. Probably no other man in the United States had such a fund of literary reminiscence and anecdote as Mr. Powell—certainly no other dispensed it with such genial and witty prodigality.

Thomas Powell was born in London in 1809 and lived in Dulwich for forty years. Here he had as neighbors, friends, or literary collaborators, most of the great Englishmen and women of letters of that time. Among these were Charles and Mary Lamb, Wordsworth, Coleridge, Southey, Leigh Hunt, Walter Savage Landor, Samuel Rogers, Sergeant Talfourd, Rev. Robert Montgomery, Trelawney (the friend of Byron and Shelley), R. H. Horne, Alfred Domett, Disraeli, "Barry Cornwall," Carlyle, Robert Browning, Douglas Jerrold, Charles Dickens and Alfred Tennyson. . . . In collaboration with Wordsworth, Leigh Hunt, R. H. Horne, and others, he prepared a volume of "Chaucer Modernized," which was published in 1841. This was followed by [dramatic and poetic publications, here listed]. . . .

Mr. Powell removed to New York in 1849. He published in this country: "The Living Authors of England," 1849; "The Living Authors of America," 1850; and "Chit-Chat, by Pierce Pungent," 1857. Mr. Powell was also the author of "The Ambassador's Daughter," a romance, and many fugitive tales and poems, printed under the *nom de plume* of "Ernest Trevor" [unlocated]. He was a contributor to the *New Quarterly Review*, the *Monthly Chronicle*, *Gentleman's Magazine*, *Fraser's Magazine*, and other British periodicals; and edited in New York: *Figaro* (1850-51); *The Lantern* (1852-55—in conjunction with John Brougham); the New York *Reveille* (1854); *Daily News*; *Young Sam*; *Frank Leslie's Magazine*, *Frank Leslie's Illustrated Newspaper*, *Frank Leslie's Chimney Corner*, and *Frank Leslie's Budget of Fun*; also "Pierce Pungent's Proverbs," and the *Hudson County Democrat*. Two of Mr. Powell's plays were acted in England [?]; and he wrote a number of burlesques for Buckley's Minstrels, in New York.

Thomas Powell, an English littérateur, who had come over from the generation of Dickens and Jerrold and transferred his habitat to this country some thirty [-eight] years ago, died on Thursday, Jan. 13, at the residence of his son-in-law, Mr. Brinkerhoof, in Newark.

It is given out that Powell immigrated with Frank Leslie, and that he had been steadily employed by him down to the present time. The impression on the mind of the writer is that Mr. Powell brought over his family and landed here independent of all obligations or other involvements.

Probably I was the first man in America connected with literature whom he called on. He recommended himself by his frequent and familiar references to distinguished English authors in a way which implied remote association with them. He specially called my attention to Robert Browning, whom Powell knew had received from me a little American volume, sending in return a copy of the "Pippa Passes," then published in pamphlet form.

Thomas Powell in many respects resembled the late William Stuart, arriving in this country not very far apart; resembling each other in personal appearance, both being bluff Englishmen, large, beef-eating and giving out the promise of good living and readiness for a "snack" at any time of day.

Powell as a matter of course fell into the Bohemian current which had just begun to acquire a heady and propontic [?] onset.

Before a long time he was hand in glove with John Brougham, Henry Stephens, the artist, and other graduates of Pfaff's beer saloon in the Broadway cellar [above Bleeker Street].

A section of these gossipers and "go-as-you-please" penwipers migrated to Nassau Street, where they set up one of the early comics, by name *The Lantern,* to which Powell was a free contributor. He was also a free partaker of the Monday lunches which were served in the office in grandiose style. A silver service was employed which was supposed to represent a part of the earnings of a great merchant, Preserved Fish, whose adopted grandson, an aspiring juvenile poet, was a confederate "Lanterner."

Mr. Powell's permanent employment in Frank Leslie's establishment commenced afterward, and was mainly given to the editing of a comic periodical, *The Budget of Fun,* with all sorts of matter, all sorts of pictures from all sorts of artists, and generally might be described as belonging to the harum-scarum school of fun-making.

In the latter process Mr. Powell's methods were peculiar; he had a special patent for raising a laugh by a misjoinder of quotations with the assorted names of authors altogether *malapropos.* For instance, he would give a line or two from "Sally in Our Alley," attaching to it the name of the Rev. Henry Ward Beecher; our "Mary Lamb," Archbishop Hughes; "Fee fo Fum, I smell the blood of an Englishman," William Cullen Bryant; and so on. This system he kept up for years.

His great delight in theatricals was Mitchell's Olympic Theatre, which he was never tired of visiting. He also was very much pleased to go on little excursions with a party of magazinents and connoisseurs. On one occasion, shortly after his arrival here, the course taken was up the North River, when one of the company remarked to Mr. Powell: "You see, sir, how prompt we are to honor the arrival among us of distinguished Englishmen," at the same time pointing to the popular riverboat, *Thomas Powell,* which was just then passing us.

Micawber rose to his height, and he was a bulky figure, readjusted his bowsprit shirtcollar and fell back several feet in a semicomatose state.

He was never known to make any direct reference to Micawber, but was able to produce very strong evidence that he had held most friendly relations with the author in whose book that character figured.

His eldest boy had had presented to him a copy of the original London edition of "The Christmas Carol." The entire inside of the first-cover page was occupied with a kind and genial notelet addressed to the lad and signed Charles Dickens. This book was brought with them to this country and exhibited as a great trophy.

Touching Micawber, if Phiz' pictures are of any authority, they represent such a person as Powell in full fig.

Furthermore, Powell was said to have been a clerk in the house of the great merchant firm from which the novel, "Dombey & Son," derived its genesis.

As a clue to the extreme business shrewdness of Dickens, it may be mentioned that when a name was required for that novel there was operating in London a firm of tailors who were plastering the walls of highways and besetting the public on every hand with the eternal iteration of their name—Dowdney & Son. Dickens, with his usual tact and readiness, caught on, and hence "Dombey & Son" availed itself of the advertising cyclone started up by the ready-money of the enterprising tailors.

The conversation of Powell was interlarded with constant allusion to his personal intercourse and conversations with the most celebrated English authors of the day.

His chief oracle was Coleridge, whom he cited as the master analyst and critic of the age. Among other pertinent Coleridgean apothegms was his assertion that "a drama was merely a ballet put in clothes." What will objurgating clerics say to that view of the matter?

Powell was himself no inconsiderable poet, and had more than once tried his hand on a play—but was summarily relegated to the colony of non-performed dramatists who banded together in London at that time and assailed managers with scholarly and impracticable Mss.

APPENDIX:
A FACSIMILE OF *PROOF (PRIVATE AND CONFIDENTIAL)*

PROOF (PRIVATE AND CONFIDENTIAL) had been called the "rarest item of Dickensiana" (Partington, 19), though only one short Dickens letter is represented in it. As but one page of this item has ever been published (by Partington, 20), a facsimile of the document, based upon the British Library copy, is herewith presented. The original in the Free Library of Philadelphia is described as "a single sheet, folded once . . . which opens so that the inside and back can be read."

Of the twenty-five copies Bradbury & Evans printed, Dickens is known to have sent out six: to Charles Kent of the London *Sun*; Samuel Phelps, the English actor; Lewis Gaylord Clark of the *Knickerbocker Magazine*; William Jerdan of the London *Literary Gazette*; Alexander Ireland of the *Manchester Examiner*; and Thomas Chapman whose firm produced most of the copy.

(PROOF.)

[PRIVATE AND CONFIDENTIAL.]

COPY OF A LETTER FROM MR. CHARLES DICKENS TO MESSRS. JOHN CHAPMAN AND CO., MERCHANTS, 2, LEADENHALL STREET, LONDON.

DEVONSHIRE TERRACE,
Thursday, 13th December, 1849.

DEAR SIRS,

I beg to call your attention to the accompanying extract, cut from an American newspaper called the "New York Tribune," in which, in a letter to Mr. Clark of New York, I describe MR. THOMAS POWELL as "a Forger and a Thief;" and I entreat the favour of your informing me whether he was employed in your house many years, and whether you detected him, at last, in any proceedings which justify that description.

I also beg you to state to me, if you can, when certain criminal charges were preferred against him before the Magistrates at Croydon.

Dear Sir,
Faithfully yours,
(Signed) CHARLES DICKENS.

MESSRS. JOHN CHAPMAN & Co.

COPY OF A LETTER FROM MESSRS. JOHN CHAPMAN AND CO., MERCHANTS, IN REPLY TO THE FOREGOING.

LONDON, 2, LEADENHALL STREET,
December 13th, 1849.

Sir,

In reply to your letter of this date, inquiring whether the description you gave of our late Clerk, MR. THOMAS POWELL, in the American newspaper call the "New York Tribune," wherein you describe him as a "forger and a thief," be correct:—

We beg to inform you that it is too painfully true, we having detected him in a series of frauds, effected both by forgery and peculation, to a large amount.

His examination before the Croydon Magistrates referred to acts committed by him subsequently to his being dismissed from our employment.

We are, Sir,
Your obedient Servants,
(Signed) JOHN CHAPMAN & Co.

CHARLES DICKENS, ESQ.

2

COPY OR A LETTER FROM DR. SOUTHWOOD SMITH TO MR. CHARLES DICKENS.

LONDON, *Dec.* 13, 1849.

MY DEAR SIR,

With reference to a Certificate which I wrote, sometime towards the close of last year, respecting the case of Mr. Thomas Powell, the fact is this: I understood that serious charges were preferred against him before the Magistrates at Croydon; but I most sincerely regarded him as a subject more fit for the lunatic asylum than the prison. I wrote a certificate to that effect, and in consequence of that certificate the charges were not persisted in, but he was taken to a lunatic asylum.

Very truly yours,

CHARLES DICKENS, ESQ. (Signed) T. SOUTHWOOD SMITH.

Extract from "The Times," 10*th January,* 1849.

EXTRAORDINARY CASE.

On Saturday, MR. SHAW, the Inspector of the P Division of Police, made a communication to the magistrates of the Croydon District, in reference to a case which has been under consideration by them for several weeks, and the circumstances connected with which are of a very singular character. It appears that more than a month back, an application was made to the magistrates for a warrant to apprehend MR. THOMAS POWELL, a gentleman who had been residing at Burgh-House, near Croydon, upon the charge of obtaining money by means of false cheques : and one was accordingly placed in the hands of Mr. Shaw. He was, however, unable to meet with the defendant ; but after the warrant had been granted a short time, Mr. Powell sent notice that he would attend at the Police Station on a certain day, and be ready to answer any charge that might be preferred against him. He accordingly attended ; and, after a preliminary inquiry, the matter was adjourned until the following Saturday ; bail being taken for the appearance of the defendant at the next bench day. When the period arrived for the second examination, Mr. Powell did not appear, but Mr. Watts, of Old Broad Street, his Solicitor, attended on his behalf, and put in a certificate signed by Dr. Southwood Smith, testifying that the defendant was in a dangerous state of illness, in fact, that he was insane, and utterly unfit to appear and undergo an examination ; and the magistrates upon this consented to allow the case to stand over for a fortnight. During this interval, it was ascertained that there were several other cases in which the person accused had obtained money by means of forged cheques, and from the information obtained by the Police, there also appeared very good reason for believing, that although the defendant was no doubt very ill, and that his brain was to some extent affected, yet that this state had been produced by artificial means—by the excessive use of opium, and resorting to the expedient of igniting charcoal in his bedroom—the object being to produce a temporary state of delirium, in the expectation by that means to evade justice. When the day appointed for the second examination arrived, the defendant again failed to surrender, but his solicitor appeared for him, and Mr. Howard, of Norfolk Street, was also present as the professional adviser of the gentlemen who had become sureties for the accused. Upon this occasion, to the surprise of the Bench, it was stated by Mr. Watts that the defendant was in a lunatic asylum, raving mad; and the certificate of the keeper of Miles's Lunatic Asylum, at Hoxton, was produced, which stated that Mr. Powell had been admitted to that establishment upon a certificate of lunacy, signed by Dr. S. Smith and Dr. Montagu Gossett. Mr. Adams, the Chairman of the Bench, expressed the surprise of the magistrates at this course of proceeding, and, at the same time, their determination not to allow the ends of justice to be defeated. The defendant's solicitor assured the Bench that he was no party to such a proceeding; and said that, by whatever means the madness of the defendant was occasioned, there could be no doubt of his being in that state, and that he was, consequently, quite unfit to undergo an examination, or to be called upon to give any answer to the charge. Mr. Howard then made an application to the Bench to discharge the recognizances of Dr. Ryan and Mr. Machell, the gentlemen who had become sureties for the defendant surrendering himself. He said they were quite willing to perform the condition they had imposed upon themselves; and, as they were prevented from doing so by the act of God, he submitted to the Bench that they were, under such circumstances, entitled to be relieved from further responsibility. MR. SUTHERLAND, one of the magistrates, in answer to the application, said that the Bench were not at all satisfied that the condition of the defendant was occasioned by the act of God ; but, on the contrary, from the information they had received, they had good reason to believe that the defendant, by the use of opium and other means, had reduced himself to his present condition, in the expectation that he would be enabled by this proceeding to evade justice. If such were the case, the illness would probably be only temporary, and under such circumstances they could not think of relieving

3

the bail from the responsibility they had incurred of producing the defendant. After some further discussion, the magistrates enlarged the recognizances of the bail, and the matter was ordered to stand over, directions being given to the Police to make the necessary inquiries for the satisfaction of the Bench. The Inspector now reported that he had been to the asylum where the accused gentleman was confined, and had been admitted to see him, and he was evidently at present in a state of insanity; but he said, he had received an assurance, that the moment his condition improved, so as to enable him to undergo an examination, he should be brought before the Bench, and he had also taken other measures to insure this result, and prevent a failure of justice. Thus the matter stands at present, the case having, from the singular nature of the proceedings connected with it, and the position in life of the defendant, created a good deal of interest.

COPY OF A LETTER from MR. JOHN ALLAN, Partner in the Firm of MESSRS. JOHN CHAPMAN AND CO., to MR. J. G. BODY, of New York, in Answer to a Letter of Advice from that Gentleman, concerning MR. THOMAS POWELL, who (as will presently appear) by means of fraudulent statements, and the use of a forged Letter of Credit on MESSRS. GEORGE VEASEY AND CO., of Quebec, in MR. ALLAN'S name, had obtained Money from MR. BODY.

LONDON, 30*th August,* 1849.

DEAR SIR,

I hasten with feelings of utter astonishment and indignation (as well as sincere regret for your sake) to acknowledge your favour of 14th inst.

Mr. Powell was formerly a clerk in my firm of John Chapman and Co., but left three years ago, having been discovered in acts of fraud and dishonesty, by which he robbed us of a large sum of money. Insanity was pleaded as his excuse, and for the sake of his family we did not prosecute him; afterwards however he was brought before the magistrates for defrauding several tradesmen; again insanity was pleaded, and he was confined for a short time in a lunatic asylum. At length he was sent out of the country by his friends, as the only hope of retrieving his character. This it appears has failed, for I find he has drawn on other parties in London, besides myself, whom, like you, he has most cruelly and wickedly deceived.

By this time he has, no doubt, left New York. I can only therefore deeply regret, that he has succeeded in practising his wicked machinations upon you. I need scarcely add, after what I have said, that every one of his representations are as false, as they are wicked.

I remain, &c.

MR. J. G. BODY (Signed) JOHN ALLAN.

EXTRACTS FROM A LETTER IN REPLY FROM MR. J. G. BODY TO MR. JOHN ALLAN.

NEW YORK, 11*th September,* 1849.

DEAR SIR,

Deceived by the representations of T. Powell, formerly in your employ, who supported his schemes by producing a Letter of Introduction from you to Messrs. George Veasey, and Co. in Quebec, (copy enclosed,) and also a credit upon the same firm for 250*l*., I was induced to address a letter to you. * * * I beg you to accept this apology for having addressed you on the subject. A much more cautious man might have been deceived by such a man as Powell, if he would be guilty of forgery. * * * * I shall be glad if you will state, for form's sake, if the letter to Messrs. George Veasey and Co., of Quebec, is, or is not, a forgery. Mr. Bell has had Powell before the Police, but we have no evidence of the forgery of your name, and he was discharged.

Very respectfully,

Your obedient servant,

JOHN ALLAN, ESQ. (Signed) J. G. BODY.

4

COPY OF A LETTER IN REPLY FROM MR. JOHN ALLAN TO MR. J. G. BODY OF NEW YORK.

London, 2, Leadenhall Street,
28*th September,* 1849.

Dear Sir,

Referring to my respects to you of the 30th ultimo, I have now to acknowledge your letter of 11th instant, which calls for a renewal of my regret on your behalf, and my astonishment (even after his former delinquencies) of Powell's daring and atrocious proceedings.

I need not add that the assumed letter of introduction to Messrs. George Veasey & Co., is a complete fabrication and forgery, of which I annex formally (in case you should require it) my declaration.

I am, dear Sir,
Very respectfully,
(Signed) JOHN ALLAN.

Mr. J. G. Body.

COPY OF THE FORMAL DECLARATION REFERRED TO.

London, 28*th*, *September*, 1849.

Sir,

In reply to your letter of the 11th instant, in which you hand me the following copy of a letter purporting to be signed by me, I beg to acquaint you that the same is a base forgery.

I am, &c.,
(Signed) JOHN ALLAN.

Mr. J. G. Body.

COPY OF MR. THOMAS POWELL'S FORGERY, ABOVE DESCRIBED.

London, 2, Leadenhall Street,
April 18*th,* 1849.

Messrs. George Veasey & Co., Quebec.

Dear Sirs,

I beg to introduce to you Mr. Powell, who is about visiting your city. His drafts upon me, to the extend to £250, will meet due honour.

He is authorised by me to enter into negotiation with your firm respecting the establishment of my son. Referring you to him on this matter, and recommending Mr. Powell to your civility,

I am, dear Sir,
Yours very truly,
JOHN ALLAN.

WORKS CITED
Books, Magazines, Journals

P designates The Pilgrim Edition of *The Letters of Charles Dickens*

Annals of Lloyd's Register of British and Foreign Shipping. London: Lloyd's Register, 1884 & 1934.

Bedi, Satya Deva. *Extradition in International Law and Practice*. Rotterdam: Bronder-Offset, 1966.

Black, Henry Campbell. *Black's Law Dictionary: Definitions of the Terms and Phrases of American and English Jurisprudence, Ancient and Modern*. New York: Lawbook Exchange, 1991.

Blainey, Ann. *The Farthing Poet: A Biography of Richard Hengist Horne, 1802-84: A Lesser Literary Lion*. London: Longmans, Green, 1968.

Blake, George. *Lloyd's Register of Shipping, 1790-1960*. London: Lloyd's Register of Shipping, 1960.

Browne, H. B. *Chapters of Whitby History: 1823-1946*. Hull & London: A. Brown & Sons, 1946.

[Browning, Robert Wiedemann Barrett], ed. *Robert Browning to Elizabeth Barrett*, 2 vols. New York & London: Harpers, 1898.

Buchanan-Brown, John. *Phiz! The Book Illustrations of Hablôt Knight Browne*. London: David & Charles, 1978.

Century Edition of the American Digest: A Complete Digest of All Reported American [Legal] Cases from the Earliest Times [1658] to 1896. St. Paul, Minnesota: West Publishing Co., 1902.

Chapman, Thomas. "Last Will and Testament." Record Keeper's Department, Principal Registry of the Family Division, Somerset House, London.

Christie, George C. and Jerry J. Phillips. *Casenotes Law Outlines*. Beverly Hills, California: Casenotes Publishing Co., 1990.

Coombs, Tony. *Tis a Mad World at Hogsdon: A Short History of Hoxton and Surrounding Area*, 2nd ed. London: Hoxton Hall in Association with the London Borough of Hackney, 1975.

Decennial Edition of the American Digest: A Complete Table of American Cases from 1658 to 1906: Table of Cases Digested in Century and Decennial Digests. St. Paul, Minnesota: West Publishing Co., 1912.

Dickens, Charles, ed. *Proof: Private and Confidential*. London: Bradbury & Evans, 1849.

Dunlap, Leslie W., ed. *The Letters of Willis Gaylord Clark and Lewis Gaylord Clark*. New York: New York Public Library, 1940.

Eckel, John C. *The First Editions of the Writings of Charles Dickens: A Bibliography*. London: Chapman & Hall, 1913. (In 1932 a revised and enlarged edition under the same title was published by Maurice Inman in New York and by Maggs Bros. in London.)

Ehrsam, Theodore G. *Major Byron: The Incredible Career of a Literary Forger*. New York: Charles S. Boesen, 1951.

Emerson, Ralph Waldo. *English Traits*, ed. Howard Mumford Jones. Cambridge, Mass.: Harvard University Press, 1966.

Fogel, Stephen F. "Leigh Hunt, Thomas Powell, and the *Florentine Tales*." *Keats-Shelley Journal*, 14 (Winter 1965), 79-87.

Forster, John. *The Life of Charles Dickens*, ed. A. J. Hoppé, 2 vols. London: Dent, 1966.

Friedman, Stanley. "Heep and Powell: Dickensian Revenge?" *Dickensian*, 90 (Spring 1994), 36-43.

Gillmor, Donald M. *Power, Publicity and the Abuse of the Libel Law*. New York: Oxford University Press, 1992.

Hill, Alan G., ed. *Letters of William Wordsworth: A New Selection*. Oxford: Clarendon Press, 1984.

[Hogarth, Georgina and Kate Perugini], eds. *Charles Dickens Edited by His Sister-in-Law and His Eldest Daughter*, 2 vols. New York: Scribner's, 1879.

Hood, Thomas L., ed. *Letters of Robert Browning Collected by Thomas J. Wise*. New Haven: Yale University Press, 1933.

Horne, R. H., ed. *A New Spirit of the Age*, 2 vols. London: Smith, Elder, 1844.

[—, ed.] *The Poems of Geoffrey Chaucer, Modernized*. London: Whittaker, 1841.

Horsman, Alan, ed. *Dombey and Son*. Oxford: Clarendon Press, 1974.

Johnson, Edgar. *Charles Dickens: His Tragedy and Triumph*, 2 vols. New York: Simon & Schuster, 1952.

Kelley, Philip and Ronald Hudson, eds. *The Brownings' Correspondence*, Vols. 1-8. Winfield, Kansas: Wedgestone Press, 1990.

Kelley, Philip and Scott Lewis, eds. *The Brownings' Correspondence*, Vol. 9. Winfield, Kansas: Wedgestone Press, 1991.

Kirkland, Caroline M. *Holidays Abroad; or, Europe from the West*, 2 vols. New York: Baker & Scribner, 1849.

Kitton, Frederic G. *Charles Dickens: His Life, Writings, and Personality*. Edinburgh: T. C. & E. C. Jack, 1902.

—. *"Phiz" (Hablot Knight Browne): A Memoir*. Reprint of 1882 ed. New York: Haskell House, 1974.

Knickerbocker Magazine. "Editor's Table," 34 (October 1849), 375; 35 (February 1850), 188; 35 (May 1850), 466; 36 (February 1851), 184.

"The Late Thomas Powell." *Frank Leslie's Illustrated Newspaper*, 63 (22 January 1887), 391.

Literary Gazette. "Anglo-American and Journalist Row." No. 1718 (22 December 1849), 928.

Literary World. "Passages from Works in Press," No. 137 (15 September 1849), 219-21; "Powell's Authors of England," No. 143 (27 October 1849), 356-58; "Powell's Authors of America," No. 157 (2 February 1850), 102-03.

Lloyd's Registry of British and Foreign Shipping. London: J. & H. Cox, 1848.

Mackenzie, R. Shelton. *Life of Charles Dickens.* Philadelphia: T. B. Peterson, 1870.

Mayer, Samuel Ralph Townshend, ed. *Letters of Elizabeth Barrett Browning Addressed to Richard Hengist Horne,* 2 vols. London: Bentley, 1877. ("My task as editor," reported Mayer in his Preface, was only to chronologize the letters. "The connecting narrative is of course from the pen of Mr. Horne.")

Moss, Carolyn J. "Origin of the Title *Dombey and Son*?" *Dickensian,* 90 (Winter 1994), 209.

Moss, Sidney P. *Charles Dickens' Quarrel with America.* Troy, New York: Whitston, 1984.

—. *Poe's Literary Battles: The Critic in the Context of His Literary Milieu.* Durham, North Carolina: Duke University Press, 1963.

— and Carolyn J. Moss. *Charles Dickens and His Chicago Relatives: A Documentary Narrative.* Troy, New York: Whitston, 1994.

Mosse, R. B. *The Parliamentary Guide: A Concise History of the Members of Both Houses of Parliament.* London: A. H. Baily & Co., 1835.

Munby, A. N. L., ed. *Letters to Leigh Hunt from His Son Vincent with Some Replies.* Cambridge: Cloanthus Press, 1934.

"The Original Micawber." *New York Mirror* (29 January 1887), 9. (An obituary of Thomas Powell.)

Partington, Wilfred. "Should a Biographer Tell?" *Atlantic Monthly,* 180 (August 1947), 56-63. (A truncated version of his article cited below.)

—. "Should a Biographer Tell? The Story of Dickens's Denunciation of Thomas Powell's Forgeries" (a two-part article). *Dickensian,* 43 (Autumn 1947), 193-200; 44 (Winter 1947/8), 14-23.

Pilgrim Edition of *The Letters of Charles Dickens,* ed. Madeline House, Graham Storey, and Kathleen Tillotson. Oxford: Clarendon Press, 1965—.

Powell, Thomas. *Chit-Chat of Humor, Wit, and Anecdote.* New York: Stringer & Townsend, 1857. (A sophisticated book of jokes, quotations, and literary anecdotes.)

—. "Leaves from My Life." *Frank Leslie's Sunday Magazine,* 20 (August-December 1886), 135-39; 193-202; 289-95; 385-89; 486-96. (Brief discussions of famous authors whom Powell met: Lamb, Coleridge, Wordsworth, Southey, Browning, Jerrold, Hunt, Lewes, and Disraeli.)

—. *The Living Authors of America: First Series.* New York: Stringer & Townsend, 1850.

—. *The Livinig Authors of England.* New York: D. and Geo. Appleton, 1849; Philadelphia: Geo. S. Appleton, 1849.

—. "A Musical Reminiscence [of Carl Maria von Weber]." *Frank Leslie's Sunday Magazine,* 20 (July 1886), 18-22.

—. *Pictures of the Living Authors of Britain.* London: Partridge & Oakey, 1851.

—. *Thomas Powell Against Hiram Fuller.* New York Superior Court (1 December 1849; 2 and 18 January 1850).

Pugh, Edwin. *The Charles Dickens Originals.* London & Edinburgh: T. N. Foulis, 1913.

Thomas, Donald. *Robert Browning: A Life Within Life*. London: Weidenfeld & Nicholson, 1982.

Whipple, Edwin Percy. *Charles Dickens: The Man and His Works*, Reprint of 1912 ed. New York: Ams Press, 1975.

Wright, Thomas. *The Life of Charles Dickens*. London: H. Jenkins, 1935.

INDEX

Symbols

CD Charles Dickens *NSA* *A New Spirit of the Age*
LAE *Living Authors of England*